ADRIANA LUNA CARLOS
Editor-In-Chief, Designer
and Co-Founder

HANNA OLIVAS
Managing Editor
& Co-Founder

NICOLE CURTIS
Director of the SRS
Magazine Division

she wins

SHE RISES
STUDIOS

ADVERTISING
OPPORTUNITIES
Info@SheRisesStudios.com

SHE WINS MAGAZINE
FEBRUARY 2025

CONTACT US
SheRisesStudios@gmail.com
www.SheRisesStudios.com

www.SheRisesStudios.com

LETTER FROM THE EDITORS

Dear Readers,

Welcome to the February 2025 edition of She Wins Magazine, where our theme, Leading with Love, celebrates the transformative power of kindness, collaboration, and courage. This month, we explore how love—when infused into our leadership, businesses, and communities—has the potential to create extraordinary change.

Our cover feature, the remarkable Randi Moxi, is the perfect embodiment of this theme. At 44, Randi boldly stepped away from a successful career in marketing and event production to pursue her passion for storytelling. She now empowers children through her books and assemblies while championing the cause of rescue animals. Randi's journey—marked by resilience, creativity, and boundless love—reminds us that it's never too late to follow our hearts and make a difference..

As we dive into this edition, you'll find empowering stories, actionable insights, and opportunities to connect with like-minded women. Explore the incredible benefits of joining the She Wins Women's Network, learn strategies for building strong, supportive communities, and discover how women across the globe are breaking barriers and uplifting one another.

At She Wins Magazine, we believe in the philosophy that Nice Girls Finish First. When women lead with authenticity, resilience, and kindness, they create ripples of empowerment that lift others. Together, we build a world where success is not a solo journey but a shared triumph.

This month, let's embrace the challenge to lead with love—in our families, our businesses, and our communities. Whether you're inspired by Randi's heartfelt advocacy, motivated to take a leap of faith in your career, or simply looking to connect with women who dream as big as you do, know that She Wins is here to uplift you every step of the way.

Together, we rise, lead, and win.

Warm regards,

Adriana Luna Carlos and Hanna Olivas
Editors of She Wins Magazine

SHE RISES STUDIOS

FENIX TV

EMPOWERHER CONTENT DAY

at

Elevate Your Brand Through Creative And Impactful Content!

EmpowerHer Content Day equips attendees with the tools and knowledge needed to craft compelling content for social media, podcasts, and videos.

FEBRUARY 22, 2025

TOTAL ACCESS TICKET: $127

WWW.SHERISESSTUDIOS.COM

Photo Credit: Daniel DuVerney

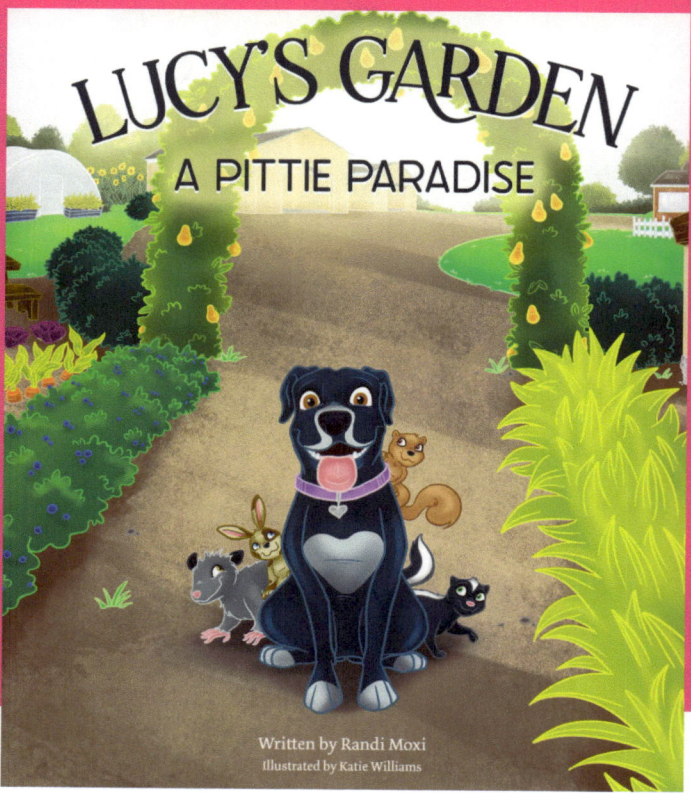

LUCY'S GARDEN
A PITTIE PARADISE

Written by Randi Moxi
Illustrated by Katie Williams

TURNING PAGES, SAVING LIVES: RANDI MOXI'S IMPACT ON KIDS AND RESCUE ANIMALS

At 44, Randi Moxi made a bold leap, transitioning from a successful career as a Marketing Director, Event Producer, and Pageant Director to becoming a children's book author and motivational speaker. This career shift, deeply rooted in her lifelong passion for storytelling, reflects not only her creative talents but also her profound commitment to making a difference for children and rescue animals.

Writing had always been a central theme in Randi's life. From composing poetry as a child to crafting plays in college and writing speeches for pageantry clients, storytelling was second nature to her. *"I was ready for a new adventure,"* Randi shared, explaining her decision to pivot. *"I'd spent my life helping others achieve their dreams, and I wanted to use my gifts to bless children and rescue dogs through the power of stories."* With support from her husband and inspiration from The Passion Test, Randi found the courage to embark on this new path.

Randi's prior roles played a pivotal part in her transition. Her experiences as a Marketing Director and Event Producer equipped her with branding expertise that became invaluable as she navigated the world of publishing. Having built brands for others, she understood how to position herself in a way that resonated with educators and school officials.

Her years as a Pageant Director and Beauty Queen also instilled in her the importance of connecting with an audience. *"Children and dogs in need have always been close to my heart,"* Randi explained. *"Creating stories with social-emotional learning elements allows me to enrich the lives of children in a way that aligns with my values."*

Randi's children's books, including the Pittie Positivity series, reflect her personal experiences and values. Each book is designed to foster emotional well-being and promote kindness, gratitude, and resilience. For example, the first book in the series focuses on the importance of sharing feelings and the power of friendship, while the second highlights community involvement, movement, and gratitude. Her third book, set to release this year, centers on the theme of serving and honoring elders.

"I want to plant the seeds for good mental health practices in children," Randi explained. *"Through the stories, I aim to cultivate qualities like love, patience, and self-control in young readers while featuring rescue dogs as the stars of the narrative."*

The inspiration behind her focus on rescue animals stems from her upbringing in an animal shelter in West Virginia. *"I witnessed the severity of the pet overpopulation crisis firsthand,"* she recalled. *"When I moved to Chicago, I saw how misunderstood and mistreated pit bull-type dogs were. These experiences shaped my desire to be a voice for animals."*

Randi's impact extends beyond the pages of her books. During school assemblies, she uses interactive storytelling to engage children while promoting compassion and understanding. Teachers have expressed gratitude for the transformative effect her stories have on students, especially those who struggle to connect.

"One little girl pulled me aside after an assembly," Randi shared. *"She whispered that she was a writer too but had never told anyone.*

Seeing me made it real for her. That moment was priceless."

Randi's commitment to rescue animals is equally impactful. She donates her book royalties to local animal rescues, ensuring her work supports the causes she cares about most. Her partnerships with independent bookstores amplify these efforts, as proceeds directly benefit nearby shelters.

Randi's personal experiences with rescue dogs also fuel her passion. She and her husband have rescued multiple pit bull mixes, including one named Brando. *"Brando was our first rescue, and he changed so many people's perceptions of the breed just by being his wonderful self,"* Randi said. *"He was good with every dog and person he met. He embodied everything amazing about pit bull-type dogs."*

These rescues inspire her books and reinforce her belief that all dogs deserve kindness and care. *"Many dogs carry trauma from past abuse, but with love and proper treatment, they can thrive,"* she noted.

Randi's journey as a children's book author has not been without obstacles. Shortly after launching her first book, she was diagnosed with breast cancer. The healing process dominated much of 2024, but Randi remained resilient.

"Switching careers at 44 was already a big change, but battling breast cancer on top of that was overwhelming," she admitted. *"Yet, it was the loneliest, loveliest time of my life. It taught me so much about myself and made me stronger in every way."*

Randi's positivity and determination allowed her to continue writing and planning for the future, even during difficult times. *"Life can bring so much awful, but I try to focus on finding the awesome in it,"* she said.

For Randi, the most rewarding part of her career is witnessing the impact her work has on others. Whether it's a child finding inspiration to write or a community coming together to support rescue animals, these moments reaffirm her mission.

Her journey from marketing professional to children's book author is a testament to the power of following one's passion. Randi's ability to combine storytelling with advocacy demonstrates how a career shift can lead to meaningful contributions to society.

As she looks ahead, Randi is excited to continue creating stories that resonate with children and championing the causes close to her heart. *"I have hope, and I know I can handle anything,"* she said. With her unwavering dedication and creative spirit, Randi Moxi is making the world a brighter place—one story at a time.

CONNECT WITH RANDI

www.instagram.com/randimoxi/profilecard
www.facebook.com/randi.moxi
www.randimoxi.com

BEAUTY FROM ASHES®

By Danette Burzlaff-Haag

In 2021, when I won the prestigious title of Mrs. Colorado – it challenged everything the world had ever told me about beauty. I am the first severely scarred woman to win a competitive state beauty pageant title. My story began 40 years earlier when, as a young girl, I survived a house explosion, leaving 70% of my body covered in disfiguring scars. In an instant, my life was changed forever. And I felt trapped inside a body that the world – and I – couldn't accept.

It took decades of fighting an internal war before I could see myself in a new light. The battles between my own self-doubt, the rejection from others, and my deep desire to feel beautiful again were in constant conflict. The stares, whispers, and judgment were never-ending, delivering blow after blow to my barely growing self-esteem. But my harshest critic was myself, offering the most lethal punches to my inner psyche. Every glance in the mirror reminded me of that fateful night and the beauty I had lost. Yet deep down, a part of me knew my story wasn't over.

Learning to silence the inner critic and embrace the inner cheerleader is a struggle we all face. Alan Cohen brilliantly said, *"If you gave your inner genius as much credence as your inner critic, you would be light years ahead of where you now stand."* No one else could do that for me, just as no one else can make that choice for you.

Spiritual growth became my anchor, helping me slowly realize that my scars were a symbol of where I had been, but I didn't have to let them dictate where I was heading. A pivotal experience in my 20s welcomed an altered view of myself, and that divine moment took place in an ordinary bathroom mirror.

For so long, I had avoided my reflection. But at this moment, I knew it was time to face it. I examined every tight, red anomaly covering my features. I bravely introduced myself to each scar so I could eventually accept them for what they were: a permanent yet powerful part of me. Determined to look even deeper than the mirror typically allows, I gazed into my spirit to find a new way to define myself and uncover beauty deep within.

My growing success also came from my ability to flip my inner script. I created and embraced the idea that life's too short not to love yourself while you're working on yourself.

Once I started paying attention to the constant stream of thoughts running through my mind, I realized how often my inner critic reared her ugly head. After all, I am responsible for rewriting those negative thoughts into something empowering.

For example, I've been stared at every day for the last 43 years. I used to interpret those stares negatively, convincing myself I was gross, ugly, and weird. After decades, I found a better way. I now choose to see my scars as God's Masterpiece of Art.

When you encounter unique artwork, you must stop and stare at it, right? My scars carry that same power, an opportunity for God to teach someone while they admire His handiwork. And I go about my day, not letting the experience steal my joy.

This creative flipping of my script has elevated my life and brought peace in moments that once crushed me. People's reactions to my scars haven't changed; what's changed is how I interpret them. Where in your life do you need a God's Masterpiece of Art kind of thinking?

Taking charge of my mindset opened the door to a better life path. Causing a once- shattered childhood dream to resurface: a calling to be in a state beauty pageant. At first, I pushed the vulnerable idea away until one powerful notion changed everything. I saw myself on a stage among countless gorgeous women but didn't see myself as *'the scarred lady'* in the middle. Looking around, I saw their life scars too. At that moment, I remembered that we all carry scars of some kind, and I knew I belonged on that stage of beauty.

I proudly showed the world my scars and their beauty. It took me three years to win that coveted crown; I had much to learn about this pageant sport. Winning the Mrs. Colorado title in 2021 wasn't just my victory. It challenged conventional beauty standards and proved that true beauty is found in resilience, strength, and grace. It was a victory for all.

As a soul-strengthening mindset coach and inspirational speaker, I've had the privilege of helping others discover beauty beneath their life scars, too. In my memoir, Beauty From Ashes: Transforming Wounds into Wisdom; Scars into Stars, I share the details of my story, not just for myself, but to light the way for others. In it, I offer the reader the comfort of knowing that life's pain and struggle can be what brings us all together to find healing from any tough circumstance.

I am living proof that beauty isn't about perfection; it's about courage, resilience, and the light we CHOOSE to shine to the world. I hope you always find beauty, no matter what ashes life may deliver.

Please visit *www.BeautyFromAshesSpeaker.com.* Danette Burzlaff-Haag, RN, BSN, Speaker, Author, Mindset Coach.

Learn more about the author at: *www.BeautyFromAshesSpeaker.com*

CONNECT WITH DANETTE

www.instagram.com/danette_beautyfromashes
www.facebook.com/danettebeautyfromashes
www.linkedin.com/in/danette-burzlaff-haag-3a28b1161

EMBRACING TRANSITION: RECLAIMING PURPOSE AND IDENTITY WITH
MONICA CONNOLLY

As we step into 2025, many of us face crossroads, wondering what's next. Whether navigating a life change or struggling with uncertainty, it's easy to feel lost. But what if this transition is your greatest opportunity for growth? What if, like me, you could embrace this moment and rediscover your true self?

I'm Monica Connolly, and my mission is to help women reclaim their identity, health, and purpose during life's transitions. My own journey began when, after nearly two decades of caregiving, juggling multiple roles, and facing a health crisis, I found myself at a turning point—one that would redefine everything.

For years, I was the sole financial provider and primary caregiver for my family. I raised two medically complex children, supported my husband through a traumatic brain injury, and worked tirelessly to keep everything together. But I neglected myself, leading to a significant health decline. I was overweight, battling chronic pain, and overwhelmed by the stress of it all.

It wasn't until a doctor's warning that I wouldn't survive unless I made drastic changes that I realized I needed to reclaim my life. My journey began with holistic wellness—losing 150 pounds, addressing trauma, and healing my body and mind through nutrition, mindfulness, and self-compassion. This journey helped me reconnect with my true identity and purpose.

Now, as a certified health and wellness coach, I'm passionate about helping women who feel lost, overwhelmed, or burnt out from life's responsibilities. Through my Rise and Thrive with Monica coaching program, I guide women on a transformative journey to reconnect with themselves and live on purpose. My approach combines holistic health, mindset transformation, and self-discovery, helping women reclaim their health and align with their purpose.

One of the tools I offer is the Thrive Blueprint, a framework that helps women reset their mindset, address their health, and ignite their purpose. It includes practical tools like journaling prompts, wellness plans, affirmations, and self-care practices—designed to support lasting change.

The work I do isn't just about physical transformation—it's about finding strength during adversity. I help women rediscover their joy, rebuild their health, and create a life aligned with their dreams. Whether it's setting boundaries, prioritizing self-care, or reclaiming their health, I empower women to take charge of their futures.

Through this work, I've witnessed profound transformations. Women who once felt stuck in their transitions have found empowerment and a renewed sense of purpose. It's a powerful reminder that no matter where you are in life, it's never too late to reinvent yourself. Life's transitions, while challenging, are also opportunities for growth. If you're navigating change, know you are not alone. There is always a way forward—sometimes, it's just about taking the first step.

I encourage you to embrace the unknown, take bold steps toward your purpose, and remember your power to transform your life. Just as I reclaimed my own, you too can rise, thrive, and live with purpose. Let's create a future that reflects your truest self.

CONNECT WITH MONICA

www.monicaconnollycoaching.com
www.facebook.com/monica.a.connolly.7
www.linkedin.com/in/mnconnolly
www.instagram.com/monicaconnollyandco

SILENCING THE INNER CRITIC AND EMBRACING YOUR UNSTOPPABLE SELF

by Dr. Shade Kolade

Have you ever stood on the edge of an opportunity, your heart pounding as that inner voice whispers, *"What if I'm not good enough?"* That voice—the relentless critic within—has a way of holding us back, turning our potential into hesitation and our dreams into distant possibilities.

For many women, self-doubt isn't fleeting; it's a persistent inner voice shaped by societal expectations, gender biases, and personal criticism. But here's the truth: while common, it doesn't have to define us.

Understanding Self-Doubt: The Hidden Challenge

Self-doubt often hides behind a mask of humility or realism, but it can sabotage even the most capable among us. For many, it manifests as imposter syndrome—the belief that despite evidence of success, you're a fraud waiting to be exposed.

Where does this self-doubt come from?

- **Societal Expectations:** Gender stereotypes that undervalue women's abilities.
- **Past Experiences:** Lingering criticism or failures that undermine confidence.
- **Unrealistic Comparisons:** Measuring yourself against unattainable standards.
- **Representation Gaps:** A lack of visible role models in leadership.

The good news? Self-doubt thrives in silence, and by acknowledging and addressing it, you can take the first step toward freedom.

Three Strategies to Silence Self-Doubt

1. Reframe Your Inner Narrative

Your thoughts shape your reality. When self-doubt surfaces, counter it with empowering beliefs:

- Replace *"I'm not good enough"* with *"I'm learning and growing every day."*
- Acknowledge that perfection is a myth—progress matters more than flawlessness.
- Treat yourself with the same compassion you'd offer a close friend.

2. Build a Support Network

You don't have to go it alone. Surround yourself with people who uplift and inspire you:

- Seek mentors who challenge and guide you.
- Connect with like-minded women who share your journey.
- Lean on a circle of allies who celebrate your victories and offer honest feedback.

3. Embrace Growth as a Journey

Turn self-doubt into fuel for development:

- View challenges as opportunities to learn, not as obstacles to avoid.
- Document your achievements in a *"success journal"* to remind yourself of your progress.
- Invest in workshops, courses, and skill-building activities that build confidence.

Sarah's Story

Sarah, a working mother of two, struggled to balance her career, family, and personal goals. Despite her accomplishments, she constantly questioned whether she was doing enough at work or home.

Determined to silence her inner critic, she started small, and kept a journal of daily wins, from professional achievements to moments of gratitude with her kids. With her mentor's guidance, Sarah applied for a leadership role she once felt unqualified for. To her surprise, she not only got the position but thrived, leading her team with confidence. Her journal of wins became a daily reminder of her growth.

Your Path to Empowerment

What would your life look like if you silenced your inner critic? Imagine the opportunities you could seize and the dreams you could bring to life.

Start today with these simple steps:

- **Pinpoint a Doubt:** Identify an area where self-doubt holds you back.
- **Log Your Wins:** Create an *"evidence list"* of your accomplishments, big and small.
- **Affirm Your Worth:** Practice daily affirmations like *"I am capable, worthy, and enough."*
- **Take Action:** Pick one area today where doubt holds you back—whether it's asking for a promotion, speaking up in a meeting, or pursuing a personal goal—and take a single bold step toward it. The journey begins with action.

The Journey to Your Unstoppable Self

Self-doubt isn't your story—it's just a chapter. Every woman you admire has faced that inner critic and chosen to rise above it. The same power resides within you. By silencing the critic and embracing your unstoppable self, you open doors to opportunities, joy, and success.

As Eleanor Roosevelt once said, *'You gain strength, courage, and confidence by every experience in which you stop to look fear in the face. You must do the thing you think you cannot do.'* Why not start today?

she wins
Women's Network

Empowering Women Entrepreneurs to Thrive Locally and Globally

Transform your life and business with access to exclusive resources, strategic networking, and unwavering support.

Benefits:
- ➢ *Strategic networking & mentorship*
- ➢ *Masterclasses & exclusive resources*
- ➢ *Member spotlights & VIP perks*

Join for just

$87/MONTH

no contracts, cancel anytime.

Start thriving today. Join She Wins Women's Network!

www.shewinswomensnetwork.com

SHINE BRIGHT: 3 STEPS TO BUILD YOUR PROFILE AND BECOME AN INDUSTRY ICON

by Lauren Clemett, The Brand Navigator

Ladies, let's be honest. How many of us feel like a *"best-kept secret"*? You pour your heart and soul into your business but shy away from self-promotion. You know you have something special to offer, but the thought of shouting it from the rooftops makes you cringe.

If this resonates, you're not alone. Many brilliant women struggle to step into the spotlight. But here's the truth: the world needs your brilliance. Your ideas, expertise, and unique perspective deserve to be seen and celebrated.

It's time to ditch the self-doubt and embrace your inner icon. Here's a simple, three-step framework – the 3R's – to guide you on your journey to profile-building success:

1. Reputation: Craft Your Expert Identity

What's your *"thing"*? What unique expertise do you bring to the table? Defining your niche is crucial for attracting clients and building a powerful reputation. Think Oprah (queen of heartfelt connection), Marie Kondo (guru of tidying), or Michelle Obama (champion of empowerment). They all have a clear *"thing"* they're known for.

To uncover yours, ask yourself:
- What are you truly passionate about?
- What problems do you solve best?
- What do you want to be known for?
- What legacy do you want to leave?

Once you've identified your *"thing,"* craft a compelling bio and build an online presence with awards and articles that reflect your expertise.

2. Recognition: Awards Credibility & Visibility

Awards are more than just shiny trophies. They're powerful symbols of credibility and expertise - even if you don't win, just being part of them provides *'branding by association'*. Imagine you're a potential client, deciding between two businesses. One boasts a string of impressive award nominations; the other doesn't. Who are you more likely to trust?

To leverage the power of awards:

- **Identify industry-specific awards:** Look for reputable awards within your niche.
- **Write winning entries:** Tell a compelling story that showcases your challenges, achievements and impact.
- **Maximise your wins:** Share your journey across your website, social media, and marketing materials - even if you don't win.

3. Results: Amplify Your Profile and Reach

Winning an award is fantastic, but the real magic happens when you leverage every part of the journey to amplify your profile regardless of the outcome. Here's how:

- **Repurpose your entry:** Transform it into valuable content like blog posts, articles, and social media content.
- **Share your journey:** Keep your audience engaged by documenting your progress, celebrating your nomination, finalist status and wins, and sharing what you learned from the process.
- **Content & Collateral:** Add the award logos to your profiles, website, email footer, presentations and proposals.

It's your time to shine. Embrace your uniqueness, step into the spotlight, and become the industry icon you were born to be. Believe me, if I can do it, anyone can. As a child, I was told I had word blindness and would never be able to read or write properly. Now, I'm a multi-award-winning author with five best-selling books.

You may not always feel confident, but you can always be brave. Take that first step, share your brilliance, and watch the world embrace you. The world is waiting to be inspired by you.

CONNECT WITH LAUREN

www.theaudaciousagency.com
www.linkedin.com/company/the-audacious-agency
www.theaudaciousagency.com/quiz-are-you-award-ready

ROSITA PEREZ: A VOICE OF RESILIENCE AND EMPOWERMENT FOR MIDLIFE WOMEN

Rosita Perez embodies the essence of transformation, strength, and joy. After a lifetime of navigating pain, self-doubt, and reinvention, she now stands as a beacon of hope for midlife women seeking purpose and authenticity. Fueled by her unwavering faith and practical tools, Rosita overcame a childhood filled with limiting beliefs and emerged as a fierce advocate and Mindset Coach for women in their midlife journey.

Her story, shaped by profound losses, divorce, and resilience, underscores the transformative power of forgiveness and healing. In her chapter, Rising from the Ashes, featured in the book She Stands Strong, Rosita offers a compelling testament to the beauty and strength found in embracing your true self. Her message to midlife women is clear: It's never too late to step boldly into the life you were meant to live. You can live UNSTOPPABLE.

Through her personal journey, Rosita shares six transformative insights that drive her forward and inspire others:

1. Personal Healing and Transformation
Rosita highlights the power of prioritizing yourself and investing in deep inner healing. By cultivating self-love and doing the necessary work to address pain, she turned her life around. Her story reminds us that transformation is possible at any age, especially when guided by faith and perseverance.

2. Embracing Forgiveness for Family Healing
Rosita's journey includes breaking generational cycles of silence and unhealthy behaviors. Through prayer, therapy, and mutual respect, she and her daughter are rewriting their family's narrative. Her experience offers a roadmap to reconciliation and healing, proving that forgiveness can pave the way for deeper connections.

3. Building a Relationship with God and Faith
Faith has been Rosita's anchor through life's storms. From overcoming abusive relationships to enduring the pain of divorce, her spiritual strength and practical tools have provided clarity and resilience. She demonstrates how a relationship with God can help rebuild your life with purpose.

4. Rising from Heartache with Purpose
Every painful experience—from the betrayal in her marriages to the loss of her mother—became an opportunity for reinvention. Rosita's story illustrates that even in the darkest moments, hope remains. With faith and action, renewal is always within reach.

5. Living Authentically at Midlife
Rosita shed the weight of self-doubt and fear to embrace her authentic self. By stepping into her power, she transformed her life and found her calling as a Mindset Coach. Today, she helps women navigate midlife challenges, reclaim their joy, and rediscover their purpose.

6. A Legacy of Love and Empowerment
As a mother and grandmother, Rosita is determined to break free from limiting beliefs and pass on lessons of self-worth, love, and boundaries. She empowers other women to do the same, showing that midlife can be a time of reinvention, connection, and profound purpose.

Rosita's journey would not have been possible without her faith in God and the unwavering support of her community of family and friends.

As a Mindset Coach, Rosita draws from her experiences of overcoming cultural norms, family expectations, and personal grief. She combines Christian principles with actionable strategies to help women conquer self-doubt, rediscover their voices, and boldly step into their true identities. Her mission is to guide women toward cultivating an unstoppable mindset and reclaiming their lives.

Rosita reminds us: *"Your journey is far from over—it's just beginning. You hold the wisdom of experience and the power to redefine your future."*

Believe it ~ Speak it ~ Be it!

CONNECT WITH ROSITA
www.movingforwardforlife.com
www.facebook.com/rositamovingforwardforlife
www.youtube.com/@unstoppablemidlife

A WORLD OF CHANGE THROUGH MUSIC WITH EMILY THORNER

In 2025, Emily Thorner is poised to take both her music and activism to new heights. As an artist and advocate, she is focused on expanding the reach of her creative work, specifically her music, which she views as both an artistic expression and a vehicle for change. One of her main goals for the year is to complete her first full album. Currently, four songs have been recorded, and Emily is eager to finish the project and share it with the world. *"Spreading the music is key this year,"* she says. *"The music can only do what I would love to see it do if it's in the hands of many…so building momentum is the main direction I'm exploring."*

Emily sees her music as a powerful form of activism. A prime example of this is her first single, *"Prayer for Peace."* The song, which combines a catchy melody with profound messages about world peace, unity, inclusion, climate change, and ending human trafficking, exemplifies the kind of change Emily hopes to inspire. As she released this song on January 1, 2025, she envisions it reaching a global audience and making a lasting impact. *"What happens if 50,000+ people are all focused together with the same intention of peace at the same time and solving the world's greatest issues?"* she asks. Emily's long-term vision is to perform her music on massive stages where large crowds can unite through song and intention. She is also exploring collaborations with organizations and groups that are dedicated to making a positive impact on the world. These collaborations could also help raise funds for important causes, further amplifying the positive influence of her music.

In addition to her music, Emily has created a healing experience through her tour, STATE OF BEING, which has already touched countless lives. This show, initially designed in 2019, is a deeply personal reflection of Emily's own healing journey. It is also a transformative experience for the audience, as the central purpose is to shift their inner state of being from the beginning to the end of the performance. Currently, the show features a mix of improvised music, monologues, and pieces written specifically for Emily. In the coming year, she plans to deepen the impact of STATE OF BEING by incorporating some of her own music into the show. This addition will create a more complete experience for the audience, combining the improvisation and written pieces with Emily's personal songs. She also envisions the show evolving with new technologies, such as the MiMu gloves, which will allow her to control music with her hands while singing. This innovation promises to take the performance to new heights, especially considering the spiritual and transformative nature of her music.

The intersection of music and advocacy is a space that Emily passionately inhabits. She believes that the most urgent global issue today is the interplay between peace and war, as well as the devastating effects of climate change. Both issues, she argues, are inextricably linked to humanity's collective consciousness.

For example, she believes sound healing could be used to alleviate thyroid issues by targeting the throat center. Emily is optimistic about the future of sound healing and encourages others to incorporate it into their lives. She sees her own music as a starting point for those looking to explore the benefits of sound healing, and she invites people to experience it through the music she will release in 2025.

Finally, Emily offers invaluable advice to anyone seeking to discover their own unique voice, whether as an artist, an advocate, or simply as a human navigating life's challenges.

She encourages individuals to trust themselves and the ideas that come to them. *"Too often people don't take action because of self-doubt or thinking that they can't do enough,"* she says. *"It DOES matter."* Emily also emphasizes the importance of inner work in finding one's voice. She believes that understanding the energetics that either block or support a person's voice is key to unlocking their full potential. Emily invites people to embark on this journey of self-discovery and empowerment through resources like her TEDx talk and the Moon Rising program. *"This is for you if you know deep down: I am called to something more,"* she affirms. Emily's journey is a testament to the transformative power of music, activism, and the courage to follow one's soul purpose, and she hopes to inspire others to do the same.

As 2025 unfolds, Emily Thorner's music, activism, and healing practices will undoubtedly continue to inspire and uplift those who encounter them. With her unwavering commitment to creating positive change, she is set to leave an indelible mark on the world.

Emily contends that war and climate change are both symptoms of a deeper issue: the low vibration of humanity's consciousness. *"We don't get a second Earth,"* she emphasizes, stressing the irreversible damage to the planet if current trends continue. She believes that the key to solving these crises lies in raising the frequency of humanity. By shifting to a higher state of consciousness, she argues, we can address global issues like war and climate change more effectively. *"In a world where more of us are at a higher frequency, there is less density and our practical solutions change,"* Emily explains. *"It's not what we do, but who we are being when we do it."* Through her music and activism, Emily hopes to inspire individuals to raise their own consciousness, ultimately creating a world where love, kindness, and togetherness prevail over division and greed.

In recent years, sound healing has gained mainstream recognition, and Emily is excited about its growing presence in healthcare and personal wellness. She believes that sound healing will continue to evolve and become more integrated into mainstream wellness practices. In fact, she has already proposed the inclusion of sound healing in private hospitals, though it has not yet been implemented. Nonetheless, Emily is hopeful that sound therapy will eventually be normalized and widely accepted as a tool for healing. *"One of my favorite scientific studies on the power of healing through sound is this,"* Emily shares, referencing a 1981 study that showed how sound frequencies could disrupt the structure of cancer cells. *"My hope is that sound healing becomes a part of preventative care and that patients are given options to supplement their treatment with sound therapy."*

As she continues to explore the potential of sound healing, Emily envisions a world where it is more accessible to the general public, not just in high-end wellness spaces. She is passionate about seeing it integrated into healthcare systems, particularly in areas where it could help address specific health issues.

RISING TOGETHER: EMPOWERING WOMEN ENTREPRENEURS THROUGH COMMUNITY AND COLLABORATION

by Jeannette Paxia

As I sat at my computer, my eyelids felt heavy with exhaustion. After a full day dedicated to my business and fulfilling all my responsibilities as a mom, I was struggling to stay awake. The kids were finally asleep, and I found myself in a familiar scenario—juggling the demands of being a single mom and an entrepreneur. Tonight, I was tackling my taxes, a task I found both confusing and frustrating. The intricacies of business write-offs eluded me, and the so-called *"simple"* instructions were anything but straightforward.

I cherished my business, as it allowed me to help others achieve their goals and find success in both life and business. It was truly a dream come true. However, as I immersed myself further into the realm of entrepreneurship, I discovered that running a business entailed much more than just the aspects I loved and excelled at. If only I could spend my days coaching, my life would be perfect. Unfortunately, there were numerous other tasks I had to tackle to ensure success, many of which I did not enjoy.

After years of trying to manage everything on my own, I realized I needed to hire help for the tasks I wasn't proficient at. It was taking me countless hours to complete these tasks, leaving me perpetually sleep-deprived and with no work-life balance. Every day was a grind, and I was on the verge of giving up on entrepreneurship. I began my search for a Virtual Assistant (VA), which itself was a time-consuming process involving hours of searching and interviewing.

Over a span of six months, I hired and trained three VAs, only for them to eventually ghost me. It was incredibly frustrating. I also hired an accountant to handle my taxes, someone who had years of experience and specialized in small businesses. Unfortunately, she made an error that ended up costing me more money. My frustration grew as the hours I spent hiring people yielded no fruitful results. Despite these setbacks, I wasn't ready to give up on my passion for coaching.

I realized that if I was facing these challenges, others must be experiencing them too. I began conversing with fellow entrepreneurs, inquiring about their hiring processes. It turned out that many of them shared my frustrations and encountered similar obstacles.

Rather than giving up, I decided to help other women entrepreneurs build their businesses by supporting woman-owned enterprises. As an empowerment coach, it made perfect sense to extend my mission of empowerment. Being a single mom, owning my own business allowed me to create a flexible schedule and be present for my children. I wanted to offer that same opportunity to other women.

I developed a directory specifically for women entrepreneurs, allowing them to list their businesses and easily find other businesses within the directory. For instance, if they needed legal support, they could simply look under the legal category, review the listed professionals, and schedule an appointment. This streamlined process saves hours of online searching before even reaching the consultation stage. The directory is accessible through my app, Women Entrepreneurs – WE Together WE Rise, and its accompanying website. The app was launched a few weeks ago, and I would love for you to join us at the start of this journey and contribute to its future success. Let me assist you in building your business.

You can download the App for both Apple and Android.

CONNECT WITH JEANNETTE

To add your business to the app
www.web.actionera.com/WomenEntrepreneurs/action-forms/0e96cc76-0062-4b6b-8c6d-3b0aa9e84353/profile
To see the app via the web go
www.web.actionera.com/WomenEntrepreneurs/directories
Join our FB Group
www.facebook.com/groups/1054747423036524

LEADING WITH LOVE:
EMBRACING YOUR SASSY, CLASSY, AND BADASSY SELF TO EMPOWER WOMEN EVERYWHERE

by Karen Rudolf

In a world where women are called to lead with grace, wisdom, and authenticity, standing out as a visionary is more than a title—it's a commitment to embody your essence and create change. Embracing your Sassy, Classy, and Badassy self, guided by love and compassion, can transform your leadership journey and empower others to do the same.

Sassy: Leading with Confidence and Love

To be sassy is to step boldly into your unique brilliance with love at the center. It's about embracing your voice, knowing your worth, and showing up authentically. Too often, women are told to dim their light, but visionaries know impact comes from authenticity and heart-centered leadership.

Leaders who command attention through presence and compassion create inclusive spaces where others feel valued. Think of a woman who steps into a room, unafraid to share her ideas with conviction. Her confidence, paired with love, invites others to trust her leadership. A sassy leader knows success isn't one-size-fits-all. She trusts her instincts, takes risks, and shows kindness—all while staying true to herself.

Classy: Leading with Wisdom and Compassion

Class is more than elegance; it's about leading with integrity, wisdom, and compassion. Classy leaders navigate challenges gracefully and make decisions aligned with their values. Consider a woman who faces a career setback. Rather than giving up, she rebuilds herself with resilience and grace, learning from her experiences and using her story to inspire others. This is the power of classy leadership—showing empathy, resilience, and strength even in adversity. Visionaries understand the importance of community. They lift others up, fostering collaboration and connection. Classy leaders create spaces where everyone thrives by balancing wisdom with compassion.

Badassy: Leading with Courage and Heart

Being badassy is about taking bold action with love and purpose. It's courageously challenging norms, breaking barriers, and pushing for change—even when it's uncomfortable. Think of women who launched businesses or led social movements despite the odds. They didn't achieve success by playing it safe. Instead, they channeled their courage into meaningful action, ensuring their impact uplifted others along the way. Badassy leaders dare to ask, *"What if?"* and take steps to bring their ideas to life. Whether it's a small initiative or a large mission, their leadership creates ripples of change that inspire those around them.

The Visionary Ripple Effect

When you combine sassy confidence, classy wisdom, and badassy courage, you become a force for change—not just for yourself but for your community. You create a ripple effect that inspires others to step into their own power and lead with love. Being a visionary isn't about having all the answers. It's about being willing to learn, evolve, and empower others along the way. Recognizing your journey—with its twists and turns—is part of a larger tapestry of change.

Lead with Love to Win

Sassy leaders trust their instincts. Classy leaders listen with empathy. Badassy leaders take bold action. By embodying your Sassy, Classy, and Badassy self, you empower others to do the same.

Ask yourself:
- How can I embrace my sassy confidence to show up authentically and lead with love?
- In what ways can I lead with classy wisdom and compassion?
- Where can I take bold, badassy action to create meaningful change while uplifting others?

Leadership isn't about perfection—it's about authenticity, courage, and heart. By stepping into your essence through love, you position yourself not just as a woman in business but as a visionary creating a better future.

Step onto your stage, share your story, and let your light shine. Nice girls finish first when they lead with love, compassion, and resilience. Together, we rise, lead, and win—because She Wins.

CONNECT WITH KAREN

www.tranquilSOULutions.com for your complimentary gift
www.linktr.ee/tranquilsoulutions
www.linkedin.com/in/tranquilsoulutions
www.facebook.com/karen.rudolf.14
www.instagram.com/tranquilsoulutions

TURNING ADVERSITY INTO GROWTH: HOW CHANELL SOLACE CULTIVATED SUCCESS FROM LIFE'S CHALLENGES

by Chanell Solace

In a world where setbacks often feel like dead-ends, Chanell Solace is rewriting the narrative, turning life's toughest moments into powerful opportunities for growth. As a mindset coach, motivational speaker, and author, Chanell has built a life centered around resilience and the belief that adversity can be fertile ground for a new beginning.

In Chanell's upcoming book, My Relationship with Dirt, readers are invited into a deeply personal journey—a story that doesn't shy away from life's messiest moments. Instead, it embraces them, highlighting the transformative power of shifting one's mindset.

From Setbacks to Stepping Stones

Chanell's story is far from conventional. From leaving behind a place once called home to facing the fears tied to becoming a coach, her journey is filled with doubt, challenge, and self-discovery.

"At one point, I felt like life was kicking me out of every comfort zone I had," Chanell reflects. *"But those moments of discomfort were pushing me toward growth, resilience, and purpose."*

The book's central message is simple yet profound: adversity isn't a roadblock; it's a stepping stone. Chanell has learned to view challenges as opportunities to find inner strength and plant the seeds of a new beginning.

The Fear of Success: An Unexpected Challenge

While many people fear failure, Chanell understands the anxiety that comes with success. *"Stepping into my role as a coach and sharing my story publicly was terrifying,"* Chanell admits. *"I kept wondering, 'What if I'm not enough?'"*

This fear isn't about doubting abilities but about facing the unknown. Success brings visibility, responsibility, and the pressure to sustain what's been achieved. It's a challenge that many high-achievers silently battle.

"Success challenges who you are and forces you to step outside of your comfort zone. But it's also an invitation to grow and embrace your potential."

Embracing Vulnerability and Rewriting Your Story

A powerful theme in Chanell's book is the idea of vulnerability as strength. Sharing the raw parts of her story was therapeutic and a way to connect with readers who may feel alone in their struggles.

"Vulnerability isn't about weakness; it's about being real," Chanell says. *"I want readers to know they are not alone in their fears and doubts. We all have them, but they don't have to define us."*

Through personal stories and reflective insights, Chanell encourages readers to face their challenges head-on, offering hope and actionable steps to turn their own dirt into fertile ground.

Advice for Those Facing Adversity

For anyone struggling with adversity, Chanell offers simple yet powerful advice: embrace the journey. *"It's okay to feel scared and have doubts,"* Chanell says. *"But don't let those feelings keep you stuck. Every challenge you face is shaping you into the person you're meant to become."*

Whether it's setting small goals, reframing negative thoughts, or taking one step at a time, Chanell emphasizes the importance of moving forward—even when the path isn't clear.

A New Beginning

With My Relationship with Dirt, Chanell not only shares a personal story of transformation but also invites readers to see their struggles as part of a larger, meaningful journey. It's a reminder that life's challenges, while daunting, are the very things that help us grow, evolve, and ultimately thrive.

"Your story isn't over," Chanell affirms. *"It's just beginning."*

INTRODUCING KAILA NIKE'S DEBUT NOVEL MYSTIQUE

Octavia, a young and dedicated mother, has worked hard to create the life she has with her two little boys after their father abandoned them years ago. She's given up hope on finding love until one night when she meets Chad, a tall, handsome, and mysterious cowboy. She instantly gravitates towards him with an uncontrollable desire. Lust at first sight. Right away she knows she wants to get to know this man, or forever wonder what if.

Chad is charming, persuasive, and mysterious. Her pull towards him is unlike anything she's ever experienced. And boy, does he look good in a stetson. He doesn't typically date, and despite his warnings of potential danger, Octavia is determined to get to know him. Their connection is too strong to deny themselves of this potential love. Whatever danger he's hinting towards, she's sure she can handle it.

Their first few months together are hot and heavy. However, flickers of doubt are cast into Octavia's mind when she is left with subtle clues of unexplainable, and sometimes frightening, paranormal activity, along with hints of potential infidelity and betrayal. But she casts it aside and buries it deep into the depths of her mind. She's in complete denial that their relationship is anything less than perfect. She loves him and believes there is nothing that can tear them apart.

That is until… She begins to learn that Chad is different. Like, really different. He'd warned her about it, but she insisted their connection was strong enough to overcome any obstacle. Ocatvia has no idea what she's really getting herself into. Chad harbours a dark secret. He claims he wants to be good for her, he even tries to prove it. But Octavia eventually begins to question if love is strong enough for him to fight the darkness, or if his true form is his ultimate prison.

This story is set on a foundation of love and heartbreak teetering on the brink of discovering an ancient forbidden and mysterious world.

About the author:
Born and raised in British Columbia, Kaila is a dedicated mother raising two wonderful sons. While she earned a diploma in social work, writing has always been her true passion. Finding solace and expression in her words, Kaila has a knack for crafting engaging narratives. She particularly loves writing poems, and *'romantasy'*. Her debut novel, Mystique, is a testament to her talent and dedication.

After gaining valuable experience working with children in a school setting, Kaila decided to pursue her lifelong dream of becoming an author. She's already begun working on the sequel to Mystique, eager to continue the captivating story she's started. Balancing her responsibilities with her writing career hasn't always been easy. Finding time to write and navigating the publishing world requires dedication and perseverance. Kaila is grateful for the unwavering support and belief she receives from her family and friends.

CONNECT WITH KAILA

www.kailanike.com
www.facebook.com/kaila.em.9
www.facebook.com/profile.php?id=61564802221645
www.instagram.com/kaila.em.9

JOIN OUR COMMUNITY

We believe the future is female and that we are better and stronger together. This group is NOT just for entrepreneurs but for women in general of all ages and from all walks of life.

www.bit.ly/srscommunitygroup

WE ARE
SHE RISES STUDIOS

We are a real-life community of women working to become the best version of themselves to change their lives and make the world a better place.

Group by Hanna J Olivas

She Rises Studios Community

🔒 Private group · 6.4K members

\+ Invite ➤ Share 👥 Joined ▾ ⌄

Discussion Featured Members Events Media Files 🔍 ⋯

Write something... **About**

BALANCING LIFE AND LEADERSHIP: THRIVING AT WORK AND HOME

by Maricel Gentile

Life is never perfectly balanced, and I'm living proof of that. I started my business, Maricel's Kitchen, in my fifties, an age when many might think about slowing down. But for me, it was the beginning of a dream I'd held close for decades. My journey wasn't one of instant success or superhero-like perfection. It's been about perserverence, embracing chaos, and finding joy in the little moments. I'm a mom of two amazing sons, Paul Martin and Paul Michael, and the wife of a supportive husband, Paul. Together, they've been my backbone and cheerleaders. When I first decided to start Maricel's Kitchen, it wasn't just my dream—it became our family's adventure. From deliveries to washing dishes when a staff member called out, my family stepped up in ways that touched my heart and strenghtend our bond.

Too often, we expect people to be superheroes, winning at everything. It's a beautiful idea but far from reality. Life isn't always balanced. There are long hours, sleepless nights, and moments when I question if I can keep going. But I've learned it's okay to step back, take a breath, and prioritize what truly matters: my family and our well-being. The parable of the big rocks is something I think about often. If you're not familiar, it's the idea that if you don't put the big rocks in first—the things that truly matter—you'll never fit them in among the smaller rocks, sand, and water of life. For me, those big rocks are making sure my cooking classes are prepped, my family has dinner, or that we have time for a family event. Most days, the beds in my house aren't made, and I'm okay with that because it's a small rock. Focusing on the big rocks ensures that the truly important things get done, even if the little things don't.

As a business owner, I don't work 9-to-5 anymore, it's a 24/7 commitment. But I've never been more passionate. There's a unique rythm to our family life that blends home, work, and business into one. It's not about separating the two but about finding ways to connect within the chaos. For us, even household chores become moments to share a laugh or catch up on each other's lives. Whether it's my husband loading the washer, my youngest son Paul Michael feeding the dog, or my oldest son Paul Martin helping with deliveries, we find connection in the everyday tasks.

One of my favorite things to say is that the idea of *"quality time"* is a fallacy without quantity time. Families need to spend time together, whether it's over lunch, dinner, or even while folding laundry. At least once a week, we make it a point to sit down for dinner as a family. It's not always extravagant—sometimes it's a simple meal—but it's time for us to laugh, share stories, and simply be together.

My oldest son, Paul Martin, runs two businesses of his own (IRL Game Shop and Miruku Bubble Tea), and my youngest, Paul Michael, is busy with college and only comes home on weekends. Even so, they both find time to contribute to our family business, whether it's working alongside me or helping their brother. My husband, Paul, works a full-time job but still manages to support me and our family. Sometimes it feels like we're all juggling a hundred things at once, but somehow, it just works. Maybe we're all a little crazy, but it's our kind of crazy.

Starting a business later in life has been a rollercoaster of emotions. There's the joy of seeing my dream come to life, the stress of managing a team, and the exhaustion of long days and nights. But there's also the incredible fullfillment of knowing that my work is making an impact—not just for my customers but for my family. My sons have learned the value of hard work, resiliance, and community, and my husband has shown me the depth of his love and support in ways I never imagined. My vision for Maricel's Kitchen has always been about more than just serving food; it's about creating a space where people can connect through the flavors and stories of Filipino and Asian cuisines. I dream of promoting Filipino food as a way to celebrate our culture and heritage, showing the world how rich and diverse it is. Beyond that, I want to share the beauty of Asian cuisine in all its forms, helping people appreciate the traditions, ingredients, and techniques that make it so special. Maricel's Kitchen is my way of bringing people together, one plate at a time, and fostering a love for these cuisines that have shaped my life and my family's story. Although next year I will turn 60, I feel as energized, if not more so, than when I was younger.

A lot of my inspiration comes from the strong women in my life, especially my mom and my Lola. My mom is a doctor and was a hospital administrator in Manila. Even now, in her eighties, she still runs her practice. Because she was so busy, my Lola raised me and taught me how to cook. But my mom always found ways to make time for me. My mom made sure to create special moments—we would go out for meals together, enjoy shopping trips, and even plan regular vacations.

My Lola was a trailblazer in her own right. In the 1950s, she came to America and happened to learn about hair perming. When she returned to the Philippines, she started a business making and selling chemicals for salons. It was truly a family effort—my mom often told us stories about when she was a kid how they'd mix chemicals, fill bottles, deliver, and still manage to get to school. My Lola and my mom were successful businesswomen long before the internet and today's opportunities for young women. They achieved so much while always prioritizing family. They weren't superheroes; they just knew how to focus on the big rocks and lean on family when the load became too heavy.

It's the same today with my family. It's not always a bed of roses. We argue, we disagree, we tease each other. But at the end of the day, we come together and make it work. Leadership, whether at work or home, thrives on love and connection. It's about showing up authentically, being willing to admit when you need help, and finding joy in the journey—even when it's messy.

Balancing life and leadership means accepting that you can't do it all, all the time. Some days, work takes precedence. Other days, it's family. And sometimes, you need to pause everything for self-care. It's a dance, not a perfect routine. For me, the key has been to stay present in the moment—whether I'm in the kitchen, at a family dinner, or simply folding towels with my husband.

If there's one thing I've learned, it's that success isn't measured by perfect balance. It's measured by the love and laughter we share along the way. So, to all the women out there juggling life, work, and family: you don't need to be a superhero. Just be you. Embrace the chaos, laugh often, and remember that it's okay to lean on your loved ones. Together, we can thrive—not because we're perfect, but because we're perfectly imperfect.

At the end of the day, our family motto might as well be: there is no work-life balance. There's just life, and we're living it to the fullest.

CONNECT WITH MARICEL

FB: @MaricelsKitchenUSA
IG: @maricelskitchenusa
TikTok: @maricelskitchenusa
www.maricelskitchen.com/cooking-classes

MULTI-GENERATIONAL AUTHOR ALLISTAR BANKS WEAVES WISDOM ACROSS GENERATIONS

The world of literature is a vibrant tapestry woven with threads of diverse voices and perspectives. Among these threads, multigenerational authors stand out, their works often reflecting a rich understanding of human experience shaped by the lessons and challenges of multiple generations. This article explores the unique contributions of author Allistar Banks, examining her motivations, the challenges she has faced, and the lasting impact her books have made on readers.

She has battled anxiety and depression and identity crisis in her relationships. She came to a deeper understanding of her trauma as she sought out guidance from her Christian roots and close pastoral friend. She was able to break free of emotional barriers and understand who she is in Christ Jesus.

Like her, multigenerational authors play a vital role in shaping our understanding of history, culture, and the human experience. By weaving together the stories of diverse generations, they create narratives that resonate with readers on a profound level, fostering empathy, understanding, and reflection. Author Allistar Banks' work offers not only entertainment but also a valuable opportunity to learn from the past and gain insight into the complexities of the present. The enduring legacy lies in her ability to connect people across time and generations, leaving behind a rich tapestry of stories that continue to inspire and educate for years to come.

CONNECT WITH ALLISTAR

www.Instagram.com/allistarthewriter
www.Facebook.com/AllistarAuthor
www.Twitter.com/AllistarBanks

PERSONAL DEVELOPMENT COMMUNITIES: COLLABORATIVE LEARNING FOR PERSONAL TRANSFORMATION

by Kathy Baldwin

Finding yourself is often seen as a lonely path. I was taught that the journey inward is one I must tackle alone, relying on determination and willpower. This perspective overlooked a profound truth, that our individual growth is intertwined with the energies we share.

Working with others helps us learn more about ourselves. By talking and sharing ideas, we see things in new ways and find out things we didn't know. Together, we can grow and understand ourselves better.

Working together helps us feel like we belong, where we can share our fears and dreams, gaining comfort and strength from others. Seeing others succeed inspires us. It helps us see new ideas and understand different people. It makes us kinder and smarter. Our actions inspire others to grow too, making the world better.

Collaboration is changing. Technology and AI are big trends with tools like video calls and project software making it easier to work together, regardless of geography. AI helps us work better together by organizing tasks and data insights. AI allows us to be more creative and strategic.

The trend is towards working together across different fields. As challenges grow, isolated methods aren't enough. Diverse teams bring fresh ideas and solutions. Virtual tools help, but building community is key. Businesses are seeing value in open collaboration, even with competitors, fostering innovation and shared purpose.

It's crucial to remember the power of human connections for our personal growth. Community and shared energies hold untapped potential. Empowerment thrives on diverse perspectives and support. By creating spaces for vulnerability and authenticity, we shed masks and embrace our true selves. Community bonds go beyond social interactions, offering wisdom and guidance. This space allows us to question beliefs, challenge limits, and unlock potential. Coming together with shared intentions amplifies our impact, creating change. Embracing community power unlocks limitless possibilities, intertwining growth and transformation.

Navigating conflicts and differing perspectives is a key challenge in any collaboration. Differences are inevitable among diverse individuals but hold potential for growth. By staying curious and actively listening, we discover insights. Embracing change and leaving comfort zones is crucial to unlock our potential. An open, growth-oriented mindset helps overcome resistance, unlocking collaboration's transformative power through shared experiences and diverse perspectives.

Charting our course with intention is a powerful force driving us toward our desired goals. Without self-knowledge, we risk losing direction and straying from authenticity, impacting not just personal growth, but community empowerment. Understanding ourselves strengthens our contribution to collective empowerment. Aligning personal and shared visions harnesses collaboration for positive change, fostering a compassionate world. Self-actualization is self-direction and self-knowledge, fueled by community support.

The need for collaborative growth is undeniable. Embracing collaborative communities is key for personal empowerment and collective progress. Our future lies in transcending physical boundaries to create virtual spaces, where diverse individuals converge to share stories, wisdom, and dreams. Within these dynamic communities, the lines between mentors and mentees will blur, as we recognize that each individual holds unique insights and valuable lessons to share. We will curate environments where knowledge flows freely, where vulnerabilities are embraced as opportunities for growth, and where collective wisdom is valued and shared.

Unlearn the Crap Community was founded on utilizing collaboration to create true personal empowerment and independence. Uncover your potential and achieve independence across all aspects of your life. Harness the power of collective wisdom and shared intentions. Together, we RiseUP, empowering one another in a supportive, thriving community.

Join the Unlearn the Crap Collaboration Community and step into your life of financial freedom, personal growth, and true empowerment.

Join Our Collaboration Community

Unlearn the Crap

We believe in a 4XWin.
A win for You, Me, Our Collaborators and most importantly a Collective WIN for all.

- Where Unlearn the Crap TV experts and community collaborate
- Unlearn disempowering crap in a supportive community
- Free and special offers for self-directed learning & self-healing
- On demand resources and live Q & A's
- Opportunties for financial independence with multiple streams of income
- Plus so much more

https://unlearnthecrap.com

FROM STRUGGLING WITH ECZEMA AND CHRONIC ILLNESS TO GLOWING SKIN: OZZIN JUN'S JOURNEY TO HEALTH AND HEALING

Every day, you wake up in pain, no matter how much sleep you get. You feel drained, with your productivity plummeting as health symptoms worsen. Skin eczema and chronic illness seem to rule your life, but you can't figure out why. Despite visiting countless doctors and trying various treatments, medications, and supplements, nothing offers lasting relief. You're sick of being sick. In today's world, discussions around longevity, biohacking, and alternative healing have become mainstream, as more people face chronic illnesses, allergies, and health conditions. The root cause often lies in a compromised immune system due to modern living, misdiagnosis, and temporary fixes that don't address the underlying issues. That's why I created Heal 365 Academy: a space where women can heal through personalized guidance and a proven blueprint for restoring health.

Go From Over 150 Symptoms to Living Symptom-Free

I spent 12 years battling skin eczema and over 150 compounding symptoms, including gut issues, unbearable period cramps, recurring UTIs, and chronic fatigue. I tried endless medications and doctor visits, but I was always left disappointed. The solutions were temporary and didn't address the root causes of my health struggles.

Everything changed when I embraced natural healing. Through detoxing, fueling my body with the right foods, and avoiding harmful triggers, I experienced a complete transformation. My eczema disappeared, my energy returned, and I regained control of my health in just a few months. This inspired me to help others who are struggling with skin eczema, gut issues and chronic fatigue.

One Thing You Can Do Today to Relieve Your Skin Eczema

You may think your skin eczema is caused by hormonal imbalance, dryness, or food allergies, but the real issue is often deeper. There are over 100 varieties of eczema and psoriasis, ranging from lupus rashes to rosacea and more. Most skin conditions originate in the liver. When the liver is exposed to toxins, especially mercury and copper. It becomes sluggish, unable to detoxify effectively.

Most toxins come from modern living: the air you breathe, the food you eat, the beverages you drink, your environment, and personal care products. It's nearly impossible to live completely toxin-free, but the goal is to reduce toxin exposure while restoring liver and gut health. Many illnesses, including autoimmune diseases, PTSD, ADHD, anxiety, insomnia, and chronic fatigue, stem from toxins stored in the liver.

One of the fastest ways to eliminate these toxins is by drinking 16-32 ounces of celery juice on an empty stomach every morning, without water. This is typically one full cup for an adult. Wait 20-30 minutes before eating breakfast. Celery juice helps to kill pathogens and toxins that trigger skin conditions and chronic illnesses. You can drink celery juice as long as you like. The goal is not to follow a quick trend but to make it part of your long-term lifestyle for lasting results.

Join Heal 365 Academy Today

Celery juice is just one step in healing skin eczema. A proper diet, avoiding trigger foods, clean supplements, and personalized detox plans tailored to your body are all essential for lasting health.

If you're tired of temporary fixes and want to reclaim your health, I invite you to join Heal 365 Academy. In my FREE Heal 365 Masterclass, I'll show you in 5 steps how to go from struggling with eczema and chronic illness to healing them at their root cause. You'll achieve the energy and health you've been searching for without endless doctor visits or harmful medications.

LEADING WITH LOVE: HOPE KHOURY'S JOURNEY OF RESILIENCE, EMPOWERMENT, AND INNOVATION

My name is Hope and I am theCOO of Go Vertical ICM and Michael & Hope. My life has been a story of resilience, reinvention and an unwavering commitment to empowering women.

When I was 28 years old, I made the biggest decision of my life, up-ended my home and comfort, my past to start a new one with my partner Michael. Driven by love, partnership, and the shared vision to create something meaningful, we embarked on a journey of our own, exploring this new world together.

Life keeps giving us a lot of fundamental moments, some moments of decision that can make us decide to stay in our comfortable zone or step out of the nest in search of a new way forward.

It was the time of my life when I was 28 when my doctor said that I had a dangerous uterine fibroid. This was not only a medical condition but rather, a wake-up call that challenged me to start a new life from scratch.

A personal struggle is now the foundation of the journey that will change young women's lives.

Getting a start was not a simple thing. I decided to leave my country, my comfort zone, and also the sense of safety that I was so used to. However, in the midst of insecurity, the love I had for myself was now greatly enhanced, and so were the love I have for my partner, Michael and the joy of the prospects of originating something out of the difficulties we experienced together. This love turned out to become the main supportive factor of the vision we shared with each other.

We became Michael & Hope together, a company defined by the values of hope, cooperation, and empathy. As time went by, Michael and I brought Go Vertical ICM into existence, targeting projects oriented towards the creation of new technology that would make life easier for everyone.

One of the most profound truths that I have experienced is that true leadership arises out of accepting one's vulnerability as a source of strength and power.

It's not the imperfectness that makes a leader; it's the strength to recover, the ability to cooperate, and the deepness of heart.

The role of a woman is multifaceted as it requires to fulfill both personal and professional duties. However, love is the key to the success of these roles; it is the love for not only others but also the love for oneself.

A ray of hope that has driven me to my current endeavor is the formulation of a botanical-based supplement that is aimed at stopping uterine fibroids at early stages. This scheme is of great personal significance to me; it was born out of my personal experiences and my desire to support women to empower them to take charge of their own health. Fibroids appear in silence, and this is what many women suffer due to the fact that they are often overlooked until they inflict substantial harm.By addressing this issue proactively, I hope to create a legacy that empowers women to make informed decisions about their well-being and future.

Compassion and kindness aren't just personal virtues, they're strategic advantages in leadership. A workplace or community built on mutual respect and collaboration thrives because everyone feels valued.

Resilience doesn't mean never falling; it means rising again, every single time. My story is one of rising, above fear, challenges, and self-doubt. It's a story of choosing to lead with love and vision, even when the road ahead was uncertain.

For every woman facing her own pivotal moment, I would like to share the below: *"You are stronger than you think, and your leadership can change lives, not just your own, but the lives of those around you. By leading with love, embracing resilience, and working collaboratively, we can create legacies that inspire others to rise and thrive"*. Because when women lead with love, we empower everyone around us to win.

CONNECT WITH HOPE

www.linkedin.com/in/hopekhoury
www.michaelandhope.com
www.govertical.co

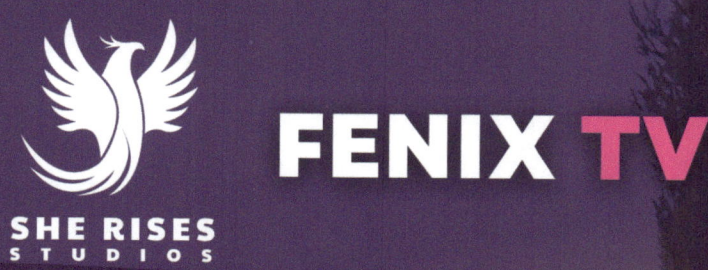

SHE RISES
STUDIOS

FENIX TV

she wins

NICE GIRLS FINISH FIRST

SHE WINS
VIRTUAL SUMMIT 2025

When: May 14–16, 2025
Where: Exclusively on FENIX TV
Tickets: $49.97

Join us for the **She Wins Virtual Summit 2025**, a 3-day event celebrating women entrepreneurs and leaders from around the world. This year's theme, **"Nice Girls Finish First,"** showcases how kindness, empathy, and integrity drive success in business and life.

What to Expect:

- Inspiring stories from women leaders.
- Expert advice on leadership, resilience, and growth.
- Strategies for thriving in business without compromising values.

BE PART OF THIS EMPOWERING MOVEMENT AND DISCOVER HOW KINDNESS LEADS TO GREATNESS!

TRANSFORMING TRAUMA INTO BEAUTY THROUGH ART

by Stephanie Dauble

Stephanie Mary Dauble is an internationally acclaimed bestselling author and principal designer renowned for her resilience and passion for reframing the narrative surrounding generational addiction and mental illness. With a background in both design and writing, Stephanie uses her unique talents to inspire others to create beauty from brokenness. Her journey has been marked by challenges, yet she embraces these experiences as opportunities for growth and transformation.

Stephanie's life story is one of resilience; she believes that navigating trauma with grit and gratitude can lead to extraordinary fulfillment. *"Every story, no matter how painful, has the potential to inspire change,"* she asserts, reminding us of the strength found in vulnerability. Through her art and writing, Stephanie invites individuals to reflect on their journeys, fostering a sense of community and connection.

In her contribution to *Plan A Life You Love*, Stephanie shares her insights on transforming adversity into empowerment. She emphasizes the importance of embracing one's story and using it as a catalyst for positive change. By weaving her experiences into her art and writing, Stephanie encourages individuals to find their voice and share their narratives, creating a sense of belonging among those who have faced similar challenges.

Stephanie's work goes beyond mere storytelling; she believes that art has the power to heal. Her designs and writings are infused with emotion and authenticity, resonating deeply with those who encounter them. Through her creative expression, Stephanie challenges societal norms and highlights the importance of vulnerability in the healing process. She invites individuals to explore their own stories and recognize the beauty that can emerge from hardship.

As a public speaker and advocate, Stephanie inspires audiences with her powerful message of resilience and transformation. Her workshops often incorporate creative exercises that encourage participants to explore their narratives and express themselves through various artistic mediums. By creating a supportive environment, Stephanie empowers individuals to embrace their creativity and reclaim their stories.

Stephanie Dauble's work is a testament to the transformative power of creativity. By sharing her story and encouraging others to embrace their narratives, she empowers individuals to reclaim their lives and create beauty from their experiences. Her belief in the healing potential of art serves as a guiding light for those seeking to navigate their challenges and find hope in their journeys.

BECOMING AN UNSTOPPABLE WOMAN: EMPOWERMENT IN ACTION

by Caroline Guirgis

In a world that often places barriers in the paths of women, becoming unstoppable means breaking through those barriers, rewriting the narrative, and embracing the challenges that shape us into stronger, more resilient individuals. The journey of empowerment is not a straight line, but a dynamic process of growth, perseverance, and self-discovery. Every woman has the power to become unstoppable, and the key lies in recognizing our inner strength, understanding our worth, and refusing to be confined by societal expectations.

Embracing Resilience

Resilience is the cornerstone of becoming unstoppable. It's the ability to rise after every fall, to keep moving forward despite the obstacles, and to maintain hope even in the face of adversity. Every woman has her own unique story of overcoming challenges, whether they stem from personal struggles, professional setbacks, or societal limitations. The common thread among all these stories is the refusal to give up.

Resilience is not about never experiencing fear or failure. It's about facing these challenges head-on and choosing to continue the journey anyway. An unstoppable woman knows that setbacks are inevitable, but they are not the end of the road. Each setback is an opportunity to learn, grow, and strengthen the resolve to keep moving forward. By embracing resilience, women empower themselves to take control of their narrative and rise above the difficulties that may try to hold them back.

Shattering Glass Ceilings

For generations, women have fought to shatter the glass ceilings that limit their potential in the workplace, in leadership, and in society.

These invisible barriers can manifest in various forms—gender bias, unequal pay, lack of representation, and more. Yet, unstoppable women continue to challenge these norms, paving the way for future generations.

One of the most inspiring aspects of becoming an unstoppable woman is recognizing that success doesn't have to follow a conventional path. Women across industries are redefining success on their own terms, from becoming entrepreneurs and business leaders to making an impact in their communities and beyond. The women who have shattered glass ceilings did so not just by their ambition but by their determination to rewrite the rules.

Their journeys remind us that we must advocate for ourselves, demand our seat at the table, and—when necessary—build new tables. An unstoppable woman knows her worth and refuses to settle for less, not just for herself but for the women who come after her.

Cultivating Confidence

Confidence is a powerful tool that fuels empowerment. It allows us to pursue our passions, speak up for what we believe in, and navigate the world with a sense of purpose. Yet, confidence doesn't always come naturally. It is cultivated through experience, self-reflection, and action.

One of the most significant ways women can cultivate confidence is by stepping out of their comfort zones. Whether it's taking on a new role at work, starting a new business venture, or simply speaking up in a meeting, every step outside the familiar strengthens our sense of self-worth and capability. When women challenge themselves, they begin to see that they are capable of far more than they once believed.

An unstoppable woman doesn't wait for validation from others; she validates herself by trusting her abilities, pursuing her goals relentlessly, and recognizing her accomplishments along the way. Building confidence isn't about arrogance or self-promotion—it's about owning who you are and standing firm in your worth.

Building a Support Network
While the journey to becoming unstoppable is often marked by personal growth, no woman becomes unstoppable on her own. Building a network of supportive individuals—whether they are friends, mentors, or colleagues—is crucial to sustaining long-term success and empowerment. These relationships provide encouragement, guidance, and opportunities for collaboration.

Women who support one another create a ripple effect, encouraging and uplifting those around them. Unstoppable women understand the power of community and use it to foster collective growth. As we rise, we bring others with us, creating a culture of empowerment that extends beyond ourselves.

The Power of Purpose
At the heart of every unstoppable woman is a sense of purpose. Purpose gives us direction, fuels our passion, and motivates us to keep moving forward, even when the journey gets tough. It's what drives women to challenge the status quo, to stand up for what they believe in, and to create lasting change in their lives and the lives of others.

Purpose is deeply personal, and it often evolves over time. What remains constant is the impact it has on shaping our decisions, actions, and priorities. Unstoppable women are guided by their purpose, knowing that they are contributing to something greater than themselves.

Becoming an unstoppable woman is not a destination but a continuous journey of self-discovery, growth, and empowerment. It's about recognizing our resilience, shattering glass ceilings, cultivating confidence, and building a network of support. Above all, it's about living with purpose, knowing that every step we take—no matter how small—brings us closer to becoming the best versions of ourselves. Unstoppable women are changing the world, and the power to do so lies within every one of us. Empowerment begins with believing in our ability to rise, thrive, and inspire others to do the same.

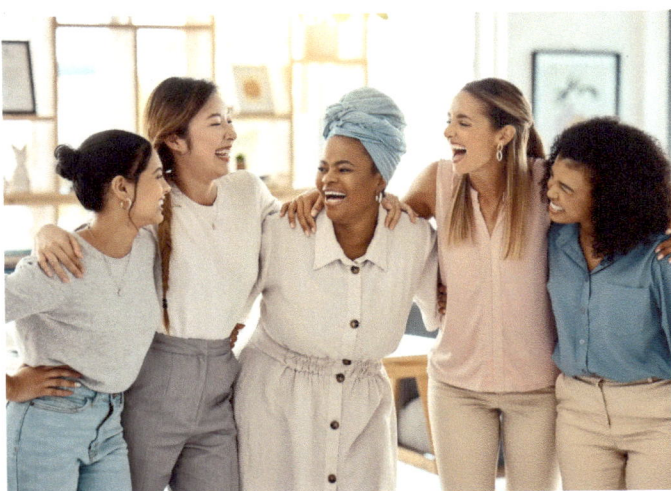

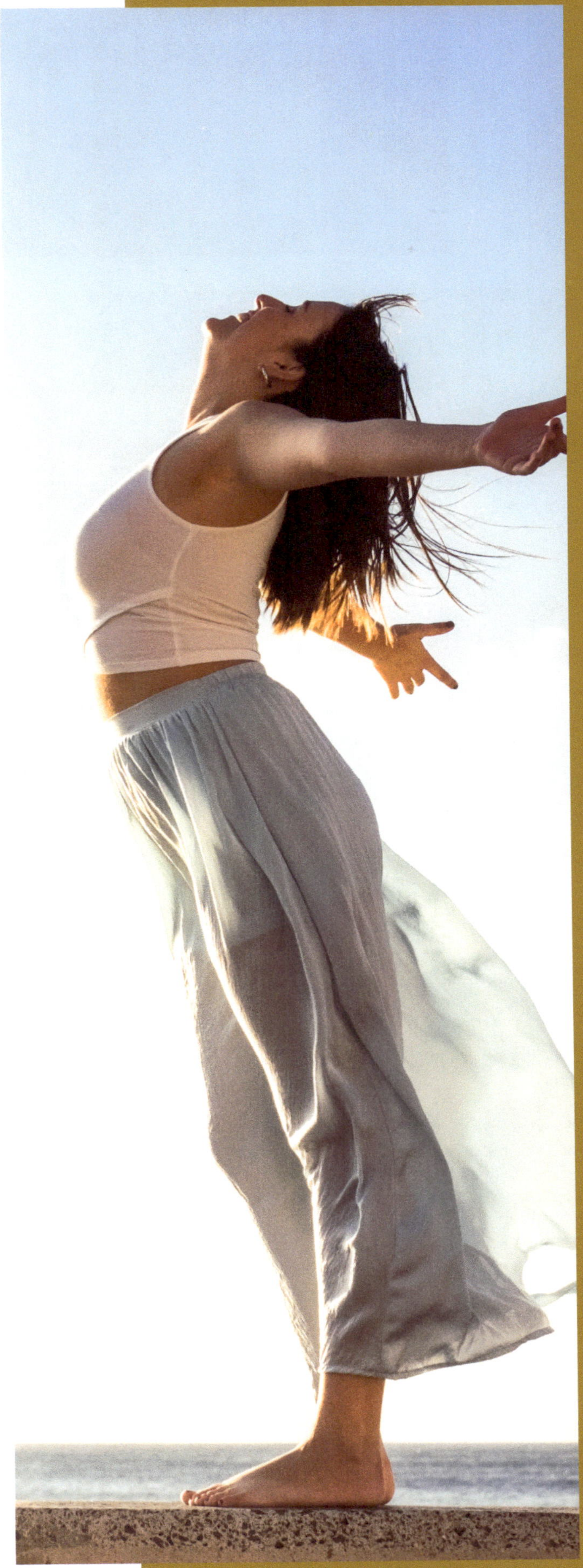

CONNECT WITH CAROLINE

www.instagram.com/carolineguirgis
www.facebook.com/caroline.guirgis.7

HEALING SOULS THROUGH THE KINTSUGI METHOD OF GRIEF RECOVERY

by Hannah Darby

I'm Hannah Darby GMBPsP SMACCPH. I run Healing With Hannah, a therapeutic holistic healing business based in both science and spirituality, helping you to navigate your own personal grief journey.

I am the founder of the Kintsugi method: I help you find your gold after grief.

So what is Kintsugi? If you are not familiar, it is the Japanese Art of rebuilding broken items, usually pottery with a clear lacquer that is dusted with gold. It uses gold to show that the item has changed, it highlights the story of the object rather than hiding its past.

How does this relate to grief? Well , when you go through grief it changes you, you feel as though your soul has been broken. Much like the broken pottery you need to rebuild your soul and learn to accept the new different you. You will not be the same again and we have to accept that it is impossible for life to return to how it was. I help you to embrace this difference and use it to empower you into a new way of thinking, no better or worse just different, much like the pottery.

We work together on your Mind, Body and Heart to heal your Soul.

Firstly we work together on the 3 M's - Mindset, Meditation & Mindfulness. I understand what's going on now, your world has changed, you feel lost and confused, unsure how to carry on, you don't feel like you did before, you feel frozen in time, unable to function.

You hear people say grief will get better with time but time isn't changing how you feel. This is because you are trying to follow someone else's journey, loss and grief affects us all differently, it's a deeply personal process. The first thing we do is a 1:1 dive deep together into your conscious mind to give you practical tools to process this loss and grief in your own way, because your way is the best for you.

Secondly we work together so you feel safe in your Body to accept your new reality. Mindset work alone will work for a time but where people get stuck is that it's difficult to keep your mind focused on your new world, we cannot control all of our thought processes, sometimes your mind will just throw you a curveball, meaning you keep trying to go back to how things were before but they can never be the same. So the next step is 1:1 work on your physical body's energetic field, to align your energy with your new reality. If you change your body's energy then your mind will start to fall into place.

Thirdly we work together on healing your heart. The reason this is important is because your heart is the place where trauma gets stored, the heart holds its own memories and is energetically 5000 times more powerful than the mind according to quantum physics. It's not just how you think, but how you feel deep inside that needs to change.

Working 1:1 releases these cords of pain, enabling you to take control back of your emotions so you can truly move forward, stepping into your new reality with confidence. This can be scary to face but I will be here with you supporting you every step of the way, I have been there myself and come out the other side. Let me be your guide on your personal loss / grief journey.

By following these 3 steps we can really heal your soul, creating a new balance, empowering you to embrace your new reality.

CONNECT WITH HANNAH

www.healingwithhannah.co.uk
www.accph.org.uk/martley/therapists-and-coaches/hannah-darby
www.instagram.com/healingwithhannahd
www.facebook.com/hannahsdarby
www.youtube.com/@HealingwithHannah-hwh

FROM CORPORATE COMFORT TO ENTREPRENEURIAL TRIUMPH: MY LEVEL-UP JOURNEY

by Marianne Schütze

Eight years ago, I stood at a crossroads. I was in a high-paying job, enjoying the comfort and stability it provided. On the surface, my career was thriving, but deep down, something was missing. I felt the pull of a greater calling, a desire to break free from the conventional path and forge my own way.

With no safety net and no Plan B, I made the bold decision to quit my job and dive headfirst into self-employment.

Leaving a secure career wasn't easy. The decision was driven by a deep-seated belief in my potential and a vision for a life where I could create my own rules.

The road ahead was uncertain, but I was determined to make it work. There were moments of doubt and fear, but I held on to a single mantra: *"If I'm going to do this, I'm going to give it everything I've got."*

Starting from scratch, I immersed myself in learning, growth, and building a foundation for my new business. It was a challenging journey—one filled with sleepless nights, countless lessons, and an unrelenting commitment to my dream. I embraced every opportunity to grow, constantly pushing myself beyond my comfort zone.

As the months turned into years, my hard work began to pay off. I transitioned from a fledgling entrepreneur to a successful online business owner, helping women across the globe to level up and transform their lives.

Recently, I took another significant step forward by launching Level Up Society (*www.levelupsociety.net*), an online community dedicated to empowering women.

Seeing the ladies in Level Up Society level up with the speed of light has been a source of immense joy for me. The impact of the material and mentorship I provide is evident in their rapid progress and transformations.

Watching them thrive and achieve their goals reinforces my belief in the power of community and support.

Today, I look back with immense pride. My journey from corporate life to entrepreneurial freedom has been nothing short of transformative. I'm now dedicated to empowering others to embark on their own level-up journeys, sharing the tools and strategies that made my success possible.

The freedom I sought has become my reality, and it's my mission to help others find their own path to freedom and fulfillment.

Every step I took was guided by the belief that if I could imagine it, I could achieve it. And while the path was never guaranteed, the certainty of my purpose kept me moving forward.

My story is a testament to the power of decision and determination. If you're standing at your own crossroads, remember: your dreams are within reach. Embrace the uncertainty, trust in yourself, and take the leap.

The world is waiting for you.

CONNECT WITH MARIANNE

www.levelupsociety.net
www.instagram.com/iammarianneschutze
www.facebook.com/iammarianneschutze

WALLOWING WINDOWS OF SOCIAL MEDIA

by *Paula J Roscoe - Grief Guru, Best Selling Author, Spiritual Coach & Therapist*

The Shift to Social Media for Grieving

Grief can be a profoundly isolating experience and before the digital age, people naturally sought the comfort of the living who would offer support and comfort, and, over time, gradually resumed their daily lives. While this process was far from perfect, it did encourage healing and moving forward. Nowadays, social media offers an endless platform for expressing grief. Grief groups have multiplied, becoming spaces where people share stories, post tributes, and receive support in the form of likes, hearts, and care emoji. Yet many of these groups explicitly discourage offering help or advice. Instead, they emphasize sharing stories and photos, reinforcing a cycle of expression without a path toward healing. Is this shift beneficial, or does it inadvertently keep people stuck in their grief?

Are Grief Groups Helping or Hurting?

The rise of these online spaces has given grieving individuals a place to vent and find community. However, I've observed a concerning trend: stories of grief that span years, even decades, with people seemingly stuck in their sorrow. It's as though these platforms have become a haven for those who have given up on life, seeking validation and attention that may have dwindled in their offline worlds. For instance, I often see posts like, *"My daughter died last night"* or *"I'm burying my son today."* While the outpouring of support from the online community is well-intentioned, I find it unsettling. In their deepest moments of grief, people turn to type messages for a virtual audience instead of seeking immediate comfort from those physically close to them. What drives this compulsion? Is it a genuine cry for help, or has it become a coping mechanism that prolongs their suffering? Or worse, is this the ONLY comfort they can find?

The Allure of Online Attention

Grief is intensely personal, yet social media has turned it into a public performance. The validation people receive online can become addictive. The attentions they find in these groups often outlast the support they get in the real world due to the reality of life.

This creates a paradox: those entrenched in their grief find an unending source of validation online, reinforcing their pain and keeping them from healing.

The danger here is that without guidance, these online communities can foster a culture of perpetual mourning, rather than a path toward recovery. Grief requires time, patience, and compassion, but indulging it indefinitely can turn it into a lifestyle, a crutch that prevents true healing.

A Call for Meaningful Support

Instead of perpetuating this cycle, why not provide grieving individuals with real, actionable support? Encouragement to step back into the world of the living, coupled with meaningful therapy and tools for coping, can make a significant difference. It's about giving people the strength and resources they need to rebuild their lives, not just a space to share their sorrow.

I understand the need for support in grief—I've been there myself. After the death of my son I faced the future alone as computers were futuristic boxes and I fought to find a way back to life, and that's what I offer my clients. I focus on practical, therapeutic sessions designed to help clients regain control of their lives and slowly climb out of the pit of despair by healing the mind, body and spirit, because all three are affected by grief. It's not about platitudes or temporary comfort; it's about real healing and a return to living.

CONNECT WITH PAULA

www.pjroscoe.co.uk
www.facebook.com/groups/healyourgriefandshineyourlight
www.facebook.com/PaulaGriefGuru
www.youtube.com/@paularoscoegriefguru

EMPATH ENTREPRENEURS: THRIVING AS A BUSINESS OWNER WHILE STAYING TRUE TO YOURSELF

by Kelle Sparta

As a woman business owner, you're already wearing a multitude of hats—leader, visionary, strategist, and motivator, to name a few. But if you're also an empath, your journey is uniquely challenging. Being highly attuned to the emotions and energy of others can be a powerful gift in business, but it also comes with hurdles that many don't talk about. Let's dive into some of these challenges and how you can navigate them to thrive, not just survive.

1. Over-Identifying with Employees, Vendors, and Clients

As an empath, you're naturally compassionate and understanding. While this helps you connect deeply with your team, vendors, and clients, it can also lead to over-identifying with their struggles. You may find yourself taking on their stress or feeling personally responsible for their well-being—even when it's not your burden to carry. In fact, for clients, this over-attachment to their outcomes can actually disempower them.

How to Manage It:
- Recognize when you're absorbing someone else's energy.
- Set clear emotional boundaries to separate your feelings from theirs.
- Practice empathy with detachment—you can care deeply without carrying their weight.

2. Bad Boundaries

Empaths often struggle with setting and maintaining boundaries, which can lead to overextending yourself or being taken advantage of. Whether it's saying *"yes"* to tasks you should delegate or allowing clients to dictate your schedule, weak boundaries can quickly drain your energy.

Solution:
Explore my free Boundaries for Empaths e-course (*https://courses.kellesparta.com/products/courses/view/1144322*) to learn actionable strategies for creating healthy boundaries that protect your energy and your time.

3. Exhaustion and Burnout

When you're constantly surrounded by people—whether it's employees, clients, or family members—your energy field can become overwhelmed. This often leads to exhaustion and burnout, especially if you're not actively managing your energy.

Proactive Steps:
- Dedicate time daily to grounding practices, such as meditation or walking in nature.
- Create a sacred space where you can recharge without interruptions.
- Learn to say *"no"* to activities and relationships that drain you.
- Practice the steps you learned in the Boundaries for Empaths course so you can keep people out of your energy field.

4. Overwhelm and Lack of Clarity

An overwhelmed empath is often a confused empath. With so many people's emotions and needs swirling around you, it's easy to lose sight of your own goals and priorities.

Tips to Reclaim Your Clarity:
- Regularly check in with yourself through journaling or mindfulness practices.
- Schedule alone time to reconnect with your inner voice.
- Prioritize tasks that align with your vision and delegate or delay the rest.

5. Perfectionism and Control Issues

Empaths often strive for perfection because they're deeply invested in how their work affects others. This can lead to micromanagement or a reluctance to hire help, even when you desperately need it.

Breaking Free:
- Remind yourself that *"done"* is often better than *"perfect."*
- Trust your team by clearly communicating expectations and empowering them to deliver.

Let go of the need to control every detail; it's okay to let others shine - even if they don't do the task exactly as you would have.

Thriving as an Empath Entrepreneur

Being an empath in business is a double-edged sword. Your ability to understand and connect with others can make you an extraordinary leader, but only if you protect your energy and create systems that support your well-being.

If you're ready to take control of your energy, set better boundaries, and avoid burnout, start by exploring my free Boundaries for Empaths e-course (*https://courses.kellesparta.com/products/courses/view/1144322*). It's the first step toward transforming your empathic gifts into your greatest entrepreneurial strengths.

You've got this—I believe in you.

CONNECT WITH KELLE

www.KelleSparta.com
www.facebook.com/kellesparta1
www.linkedin.com/in/kellesparta
www.instagram.com/kellesparta
www.tiktok.com/@kellesparta
www.SpiritSherpaPodcast.com
www.SpiritGuidesPodcast.com
www.youtube.com/channel/UC0jXbllhVIDcHRq MSQpR2DQ
https://learn.kellesparta.com/shadowworkquiz

THE #1 SABOTEUR OF SCALING TO 7 FIGURES: WHY FEAR IS YOUR GREATEST ALLY

by Stephanie Zito

Success is an electrifying journey, but it's also a confronting one. For entrepreneurs scaling to seven figures, an inevitable roadblock appears like clockwork: fear. This fear isn't the problem; it's your greatest guide. It shows up precisely when you're ready to step into a bigger version of yourself, signaling you're on the brink of a breakthrough.

Most of us try to push past fear, believing we can outwork or outrun it. But the reality is, fear is there to provide information, to remind us that we're approaching uncharted territory. It's not a saboteur—it's a messenger.

Fear is Information
When fear shows up as you're scaling, it's an invitation to go deeper, to release the limiting beliefs that are no longer aligned with where you're heading. The biggest mistake entrepreneurs make is trying to sidestep or suppress that fear, thinking they can simply hustle their way through it. But in doing so, you miss the opportunity for growth.

In my own experience, this truth became undeniable when my family and I made a major life decision last year. We gave up our ideal mortgage rate in exchange for more space to entertain friends and create a home that fit the vision we had for our family. That move also gave me the opportunity to uplevel my business—transitioning from working at my kitchen table to having a gorgeous office of my own. With that shift, I made a decision: I wasn't going to ride the rollercoaster of $10k months anymore. I committed to hitting six figures in six months.

As soon as I set that goal, my limiting beliefs reared their heads. The voices of doubt, of sabotage, of *'what if it's too much'* came flooding in. But as a hypnotherapist, I had the tools to navigate this moment. I understood that this wasn't just fear for fear's sake—this was the old version of me clinging to safety, trying to keep me small.

Clearing Limiting Beliefs: The Real Uplevel
This is where the power of clearing limiting beliefs comes in. The Proctor Gallagher Institute states that 5% of money success is strategy, and 95% is mindset. Most people get stuck because they think more strategy is the answer, but what's really needed is an internal shift. Through techniques like hypnosis, you can remove the barriers that

sabotage your success and recalibrate your mindset so you're not working against yourself.

Fear and sabotage are mechanisms designed to keep you safe, to preserve the status quo. They aren't there to stop you; they're there to show you what needs to be released. Hypnosis is one of the most effective ways to address these deep-seated beliefs. It doesn't just help you *'manage'* fear—it transforms it. When your mind feels safe to move forward, the strategy you implement will be exponentially more effective because you're no longer energetically holding yourself back.

In my case, once I used hypnosis to clear those limiting beliefs, everything shifted. The fear dissolved, and what was left was a clear, focused determination. My business went from the inconsistency of $10k months to achieving six figures in a fraction of the time. It wasn't because of some new marketing tactic or a complicated funnel. It was because I addressed the root cause—my internal resistance.

From Saboteur to Strategy
The irony is that the very thing we think is holding us back—fear, self-doubt, sabotage—is what we need to lean into. If you're feeling that resistance as you scale, take it as a sign you're right on track. Fear shows up because it's trying to protect the old version of you. But to reach that next level, to break through to seven figures, you need to release what no longer serves you.

By investing in clearing your limiting beliefs, through tools like hypnosis, you're not just *'getting rid of fear.'* You're transforming how you operate in your business. You stop working against yourself and start moving in alignment with your highest potential. And when that happens, success isn't just a possibility—it's inevitable.

The bottom line? Don't fear fear. Welcome it, use it as the catalyst it's meant to be, and let it propel you to your next level.

INSPIRED. EMPOWERED.
UNSTOPPABLE.

CORE TRUTH: TAPPING INTO AUTHENTICITY

by Tammy Cameron

The Formula We Know

Get educated. Find a job. Rent an apartment. Get married. Buy a house. Have a baby. Take a vacation. Celebrate the holidays. This is supposed to be the recipe for success and a fulfilling life; it is what society guides us to do. Beyond this, we are to work a good job, be a stellar role model, volunteer, donate, and advance in our chosen career. Next, we are to retire, garden, golf, downsize possessions, travel, and *"enjoy life."* If this were a one size fits all formula, everyone would be happy in every stage along this journey.

Instead, we see and experience struggle, challenges, and discontent at select stages. Some events do not go as planned. Occasionally, we do not agree with the plan. Often, the timeline does not align with our wish.

The Formula We Learn

The anthology She Stands Strong: 30 Personal Stories of Strength and Resilience introduces thirty women who have all faced such situations. They faced their obstacles with a courage like no other, understanding one core constant - time. Time will pass and life will unfold in the chaos around us. Setbacks will come in many forms. It is our responsibility to ourselves to find the beauty, uncover the lessons, and emerge stronger than ever before.

Strip away the external influences. Quiet the voices of doubt and criticism that attempt to infiltrate your thoughts. Eliminate the worry over judgement. Find your stillness within. What do you want? This is your moment of truth, power, and choice, and it is YOUR choice.

The Invitation

Join the women who have stood before you and those who will stand after you. Build your unstoppable skillset. Bring your gifts to the world and show us the uniqueness that is YOU.

The Process

- **Step One – TIME - Carve out time.** Life is busy. Get up an hour early. Sleep an hour late. Reduce your beauty or fitness routine. Order meals. Employ a personal shopper. Make the choice that is best for you but carve out time.

- **Step Two – INFLUENCE - Identify and strip away external influences.** Which thoughts belong to others, and which are yours?
- **Step Three – CORE - Connect to your core truth.** Find quiet. Close your eyes and breathe deeply. What is the most important thought coming forward?
- **Step Four – PRIORITIZE - Curate your priorities.** You may be flooded with an abundance of thoughts. Breathe slowly and deeply. What is the most important thing today? Now? In this moment? Put your focus here.
- **Step Five – ACT - Authentically act.** What step can you take today and now to remain aligned with your core priority?

Tips

This may not be easy. Easy is watching television and engaging in routine activities that we already know and do comfortably. An unstoppable skillset requires growth and transformation which take effort. You are invited to stretch beyond the familiar routine to your true authentic core. You know it deep down in your being. It calls to you. Be gentle with yourself. Exercise self-love and compassion along with forgiveness. Encourage yourself. Small and steady gains are perfect! Do not compare yourself to others; we all have our unique paths.

Compare yourself yesterday to yourself today: stronger, bolder, and more aware. Be proud of your efforts and action steps. Feel the delight of your choices. Feel your sleep improve! Yes, with authentic living comes GOOD sleep. You are unstoppable. Chart your happy, healthy, success formula because I know you can!

Final Words

What we know + what we learn & share = a better world.

FROM GRIEF TO GROWTH: HOW LOSS SHAPED MY PURPOSE AND PASSION

by Lisa Heacock

I moved to the UK in 2005 from America. I always dreaded *"the phone call."* The call that someone you loved had died. Living four thousand miles away. That call came in January 2018. My niece passed away from a hereditary illness. One week later my mom phoned me to say my dad had been diagnosed with brain cancer. I quit my job and moved back to Seattle to care for my dying father and my heartbroken mother. Seven months later he passed away. I was deep in grief and exhaustion. I did return home to the UK. Leaving my mother was incredibly difficult but I knew she had my brother and all her amazing friends.

Several months later my mom came to visit. We had a wonderful time together. Two months later it was time to drop her off at the Manchester airport. She was crying and I was trying to keep it together. I had no idea that would be the last time I would hug my mom. She passed away in her sleep four months later. Shocked and devastated, an orphan at 49.

Between 2018 and 2019, I had lost twelve loved ones, friends and friends' children but nothing could have prepared me for the worst phone call of my life. Two months after my mom passed, I received a call in the middle of the night telling me my twenty-four-year-old son-in-law Jack passed away from a fall. I could not believe what I was hearing. The devastation of losing Jack felt too much to bear.

How do you grieve the loss of so many people. Who do you grieve first. How do carry your grief and the grief of others. Grief is difficult to navigate and compound grief is like a big ball of messy, painful, string that you do not want to pull on in fear it all unravels and you can never put it back together.

I knew that I could not do this alone. I hired a bereavement counsellor. I sought out other healing modalities such as yoga, breathwork, meditation, sound bath classes, mediums, energy healing. I tried everything.

A year later I began asking myself, *'Now what?'* I knew this was my reality but what was I going to do. I hired a Life Coach.
When you lose loved ones through death, it changes you. It changed the trajectory of my life. I understood at a cellular level that life is short and fragile and you better not waste it.

I began to look at areas of my life that I was unhappy and unfulfilled. My husband of twenty-eight years and I divorced amicably.

I studied to become a Certified and Accredited Life Coach and Certified Grief Educator. I now share my story in hopes to help those who are grieving any type of loss and educate those who are supporting grieving loved ones.

I am living proof you can fully live and fully grieve.
In March 2023, I was diagnosed with breast cancer. I had a mastectomy and chose to have the healthy one removed. I now live flat and free.

Whilst facing breast cancer, I was able to use some of the same tools I used during my season of extreme loss. I was able to remain positive, work on my mindset, rest, recover, keep my sense of humour and hopefully inspire a few people along the way.

I have created a life of passion and purpose around my pain and now I help others do the same.

CONNECT WITH LISA

www.holisticlifecoaching.org.uk
www.facebook.com/lisa.messexheacock
www.instagram.com/holistic_coach_lisa
www.facebook.com/holisticlifecoachingwithlisamarie

GET A COPY TODAY!

www.amazon.com/Her-Unseen-Battle-Accompanied-Affirmations-ebook/dp/B0DNKGBWB6

Discover a celebration of courage and resilience in Her Unseen Battle. This inspiring book shines a light on the silent struggles women face and the strength it takes to overcome them. Through raw, unfiltered stories, women from diverse walks of life share their journeys—navigating loss, breaking free from self-doubt, challenging societal norms, and battling invisible struggles like mental health.

Each story is accompanied by practical tips, empowering affirmations, and actionable steps to help you build resilience, find healing, and reclaim your power.

With tools like mindfulness exercises, self-care strategies, and affirmations for self-love, this book offers guidance to support your own path to transformation.

Her Unseen Battle reminds us all that no struggle is too small or unseen to matter. It's a testament to the strength of the human spirit and an invitation to embrace your vulnerabilities, rise above challenges, and step into your true potential.

Your battle is seen. Your pain is valid. And within you lies the power to heal and thrive.

From Working Mom to Empowered Mompreneur: The Resilience, Determination, and Inspiring Journey of Anisa Crespo

I'm Anisa Crespo, the Founder of My Mompreneur Studio! My entrepreneurial journey began in 2020 amidst the chaos of the global pandemic when my twins were born. Navigating the challenges of motherhood alone while my husband served as an essential worker, I delved into online skills and self-taught entrepreneurship, venturing into various industries, including but not limited to, digital marketing and real estate investment. Despite juggling newborns and a demanding full-time job, I pursued my passion relentlessly.

In 2022, my husband and I moved to Florida, where I embraced my mission to empower women fully. Faced with a melanoma diagnosis and the strain of balancing motherhood, work, and business, I had a spiritual awakening, dedicating myself to my core values of faith, family, health, wealth, and freedom. Throughout my life, I've faced innumerable traumas that could have defined me negatively, but instead, I chose to rise above them. Every hardship I've endured has become a lesson, fueling my passion to help other women navigate their own journeys and challenges. By sharing my story and offering support, I empower women to reclaim their strength and rewrite their narratives.

In 2024, I left my six-figure corporate job in a male-dominated industry to pursue my true calling: helping women, moms in particular.

Through My Mompreneur Studio, I offer mentorship, coaching, a podcast platform to amplify voices of women, and a space for women to pursue their dreams. My latest project, *"Empower Her Story,"* with She Rises Studios embodies my vision of uplifting women worldwide. Growing up, I witnessed my mother struggling as a single parent, instilling in me a sense of determination and grit. Despite setbacks and obstacles, I refused to succumb to despair, viewing each challenge as an opportunity for growth and learning.

The birth of my twins thrust me into the role of motherhood during the pandemic. Balancing parenthood with career aspirations seemed daunting, but drawing upon the lessons from my mother, I embarked on a journey of self-discovery and empowerment.

Navigating the intricacies of online marketing and real estate investment, I faced a steep learning curve. Yet, with each obstacle, I refused to falter, embracing challenges as opportunities for growth and learning. Through sheer determination and perseverance, I carved out a niche in entrepreneurship.

The journey has been transformative, pushing me beyond my limits and forcing me to confront my deepest fears. Today, as I reflect on my journey, I am filled with gratitude for the experiences that have shaped me. Through My Mompreneur Studio and other initiatives, I am committed to making a lasting impact on the lives of women globally. Together, let us rise above our challenges and embrace our limitless potential.

FROM AWARD-WINNING EVENT MANAGEMENT TO ADDICTION: MY JOURNEY OF RECOVERY AND RESILIENCE

by Connie Paglianiti

For over 40 years, I thrived in the fast-paced world of event management, creating unforgettable experiences with celebrities like Susan Sarandon, Sophia Loren, Jane Seymour, and Goldie Hawn. From intimate charity galas to large-scale festivals for thousands, my work earned state awards in Victoria, including for the La Dolce Italia Carnevale Masquerade Ball, a finalist for Best New Event. It was a glamorous, high-pressure life. But behind the scenes, I was battling a personal struggle that would eventually threaten everything I had built.

When Success Collides with Adversity

My journey took a dramatic turn when a business deal went horribly wrong. I was deceived by someone I trusted, and in an attempt to recover my losses, I turned to gambling. What began as a desperate effort to regain control spiraled into a destructive addiction. My life, once defined by successful events and accolades, began to unravel.

The losses weren't just financial—they were deeply emotional and spiritual. I made choices I deeply regret, choices that eventually landed me in prison for two and a half years. The shame, guilt, and fear of losing everything I had built were suffocating. When I was released, I spent another two and a half years isolating myself, convinced my life and career were over.

Rebuilding From the Ground Up

Recovery from addiction isn't easy, and my journey was no exception. But through therapy, support groups, and the strength of the people around me, I began to rebuild my life.

One of the most powerful lessons I learned along the way is that no matter how successful or in control you seem, adversity can strike anyone at any time. The key is how you respond to it.

This realization has been invaluable in my professional comeback. When I returned to the world of event management, I had a renewed sense of purpose. My career wasn't just about executing flawless events anymore—it became about championing causes, inspiring change, and giving back to the communities that supported me. This shift in focus gave me not only personal fulfillment but also a new way to lead with authenticity and purpose.

Leadership Through Reinvention

In business, challenges can feel overwhelming, but they often provide opportunities to innovate and grow. My setback led me to re-evaluate how I approached my career. Instead of seeing myself only as an event manager, I saw an opportunity to become an educator and mentor.

I've now written eBooks on event management and developed online courses to train the next generation of event professionals. This has allowed me to scale my expertise and create multiple streams of income. These courses don't just focus on logistics and execution; I emphasize the importance of ethics, sustainability, and resilience—qualities that are essential for long-term business success.

Practical Lessons for Entrepreneurs and Leaders

Through my journey, I've learned that resilience and adaptability are critical for thriving in the modern business world. Here are some key insights that have helped me rebuild my career and could serve as valuable lessons for entrepreneurs and professionals alike:

1. **Learn from Failure, Don't Fear It:** Setbacks are inevitable in business. What matters is how you respond to them. View failures as opportunities for learning and innovation. After my business collapsed, I had to pivot, leveraging my experience in a new way—through education and public speaking.

2. **Diversify Your Skills and Revenue Streams:** Don't limit yourself to one career path or business model. While my core expertise remains in event management, diversifying into eBooks and online courses has allowed me to reach new markets and stabilize my income.

3. **Lead with Purpose:** Today's customers and clients are more socially conscious than ever. Leading with a mission that aligns with your values, whether through supporting a cause or ensuring ethical practices in your business, can give you a unique edge.

4. **Invest in Your Personal Growth:** No matter how experienced or accomplished you are, there's always room for personal and professional development. My journey through addiction recovery was also a journey of self-discovery. Learning to embrace vulnerability and seek help when needed made me a better leader.

Looking Forward

It's been a long road from the pinnacle of event management to addiction, prison, and finally, recovery. But the journey has taught me that success isn't just about accolades and achievements—it's about resilience, self-compassion, and leading with integrity.

Today, I'm proud of the work I've done and the person I've become. My story is one of redemption and reinvention, and if it can offer hope and inspiration to others, then every challenge I faced was worth it. I continue to manage events, speak about addiction recovery, and teach the next generation of event professionals how to succeed—ethically and sustainably.

The business world is fast-paced and ever-evolving, but if you stay true to your values and embrace the lessons in adversity, you can find both personal fulfillment and professional success.

CONNECT WITH CONNIE

www.conniepaglianiti.com
www.linkedin.com/in/conniepaglianiti
www.instagram.com/conniempaglianiti
www.facebook.com/ConniePaglianiti
www.facebook.com/profile.php?id=61560347468477

MINDSET.

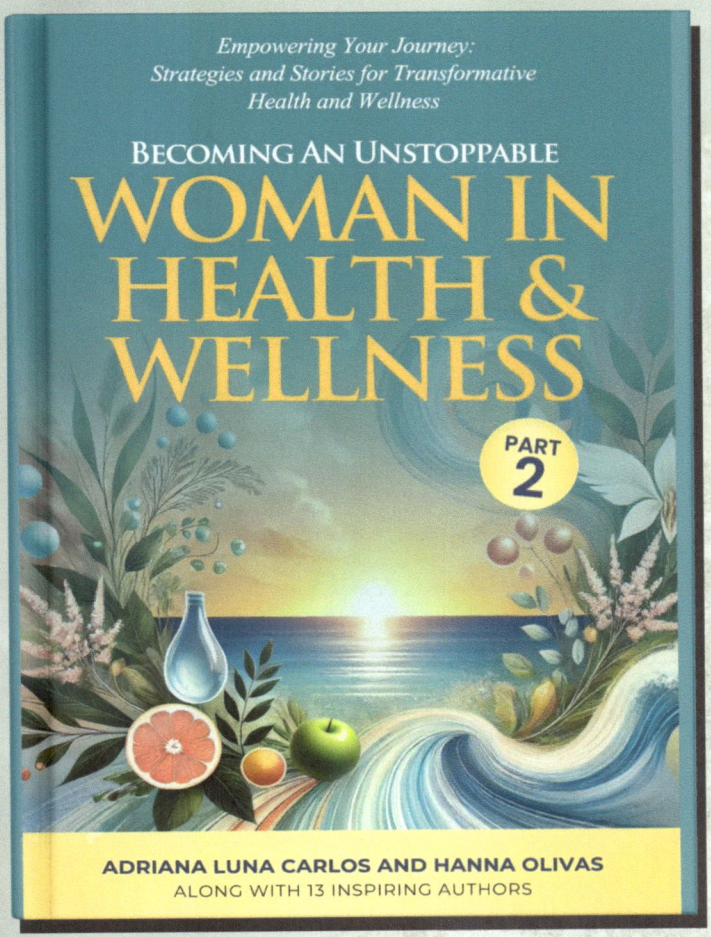

SHE RISES STUDIOS

amazon

GRAB YOUR COPY NOW!

www.amazon.com/Becoming-Unstoppable-Woman-Health-Wellness/dp/1964619688

Becoming an Unstoppable Woman in Health & Wellness – Part 2: Empowering Your Journey is a transformative anthology of stories, wisdom, and strategies to inspire your health journey. Featuring remarkable women who've overcome challenges and embraced resilience, this book offers personal insights and practical advice to help you cultivate a healthier mindset, balanced nutrition, effective fitness routines, and self-care practices.

Let these powerful accounts empower you to take charge of your well-being, embrace self-love, and unlock your full potential. **Your journey to becoming an unstoppable woman starts here—take the first step today!**

A JOURNEY TOWARDS SELF-LOVE

by Deborah Corsetti

In the world that demands perfection and comparison, the concept of self-love can be quite difficult. Yet, throughout my journey, I realized that self-love is the foundation in which we can build a life of happiness, fulfillment, and deepen our connection, not only towards others, but most importantly with ourselves.

Embark with me today, on the journey of self-love, where we not only nurture our own well-being, but contribute to the journey towards embracing our own self-worth.

Self love is not just about affirmations and mantras, but it is an absolute necessity for us to build a strong foundation to be able to move through difficult and challenging times in our lives with grace and resilience.

I am a strong advocate for self-love for so many reasons, but here's a few:

Self-love is the basis of fulfilment in our lives. It's recognizing and embracing our unique flaws and all. When we truly love ourselves, we're better equipped to pursue our passions, set goals for ourselves, and cultivate a sense of purpose that resonates from deep within.

Self love isn't just about the self, but it's about how we express ourselves to the world as well. When we love ourselves, we radiate positivity. Self love enables us to be authentic, setting an example for and inspiring those around us, to discover their own journey of self discovery and self acceptance.

When we love ourselves, it is reflected in the way we carry ourselves, the way we speak, and the way we interact with the world. When we love ourselves, we exude confidence and resilience. We become the creators of our reality and draw people and new opportunities towards us .

Loving ourselves is an act of giving not just to ourselves, but to the greater good. When we prioritize our own well-being and happiness, we become better equipped to serve others and make a positive impact on the world around us.

Lastly, I truly believe that self love is the key to empowerment. It allows us to move forward on our journey towards becoming the best versions of ourselves. When we love ourselves unconditionally, we break free from the shackles of self doubts and fear and move towards embracing our own self-worth.

Self-love isn't selfish it's essential!
* Essential for resilience in challenging moments.
* Essential for authentic connections.
* Essential for our emotional well-being and so much more.

Here are some tips for starting YOUR self love journey:

1. **Practice self compassion:** treat yourself with the same kindness and understanding you would offer to a dear friend. Be gentle with yourself, especially in times of struggle or setback.

2. **Practice gratitude:** being grateful for the small things that are already in your life can significantly improve your overall well-being. Appreciating the little things in life can lead to greater happiness.

3. **Set boundaries:** Learn to say no to things that drain your energy or compromise your well-being. Prioritize activities, and relationships that nurse your soul and align with your values.

4. **Celebrate your strengths:** Embrace your unique talents, skills, and qualities. Celebrate your successes and acknowledge the value you bring to the world.

5. **Cultivate mindfulness:** Take the time each day to quiet your mind, connect with your breath and tune into the present moment. Practice mindfulness meditation or simply engage in activities that bring you joy and peace.

6. **Seek support:** Don't be afraid to reach out to friends, family, or a life coach for guidance on your self love journey. Surround yourself with people who uplift and encourage you to be your authentic self.

In conclusion, self-love isn't a luxury… It's a necessity for living a life of fulfillment, happiness, and empowerment.

By prioritizing, our own well-being and fully embracing our worth, we lay the foundation for a brighter, more compassionate world-a world filled with love, acceptance, and endless possibilities. So today, and every day, choose to love yourself completely and unapologetically.

Your journey to self-love starts NOW!

CONNECT WITH DEBORAH

Deb.corsetti on instagram
DCs Mindful Zone on Facebook
DC self guidance on Facebook

HUMAN CONNECTION AND EMOTIONAL REGULATION IN THE AGE OF AI

by Ammie Michaels

As a certified mediator and facilitator in Human Resources, I spend my days working closely with individuals and teams to navigate the complexities of communication, collaboration, and connection. With the rapid advancement of artificial intelligence and technology, I have become increasingly concerned about the growing disconnect in human interactions. This concern is deeply rooted in both my professional experiences and my personal interactions within the business community with more companies replacing humans with computers.

The Disconnect in the Digital Age

The increasing adoption of artificial intelligence (AI) has brought numerous benefits, including increased efficiency, innovative solutions, and a transformed workplace. However, it has also introduced significant challenges, particularly in the realm of human connection. More than ever, people are spending their lives behind screens, often at the expense of face-to-face interactions. This shift is particularly pronounced among the newest generations, who are growing up in a digital-first world. The consequences of this digital immersion are becoming increasingly apparent: a decline in basic social skills and a worrying erosion of emotional intelligence.

The Role of Emotional Intelligence

Emotional intelligence (EI) – the ability to understand, manage, and express emotions effectively – is crucial for meaningful human connection. It underpins our capacity for empathy, communication, and conflict resolution. Without it, our interactions can become superficial, leading to misunderstandings, frustration, and isolation. In my work, I frequently encounter teams struggling with these very issues. Technology, while incredibly useful, cannot replace the nuanced, empathetic interactions that build trust and foster genuine relationships.

My Mission

My mission is to bridge this growing gap by fostering true human connection and interaction. Through my workshops, mediation sessions, and team-building activities, I strive to create environments where individuals can connect on a deeper level. These spaces encourage open dialogue, active listening, and emotional honesty. I have witnessed firsthand the transformative power of these interactions – they not only enhance workplace productivity but also contribute to a more fulfilling, connected, and joyful life.

Personal Journey

My commitment to this mission is deeply personal. In EmpowerHER Story, I detail my own journey to discovering joy and happiness through the deepening of my own of emotional intelligence and adoption of self-regulation practices. This journey was not easy; it required introspection, vulnerability, and a willingness to confront my own emotional disconnection. But it was through this process that I found a profound sense of fulfillment and a renewed capacity for connection. This experience has reinforced my belief in the importance of emotional intelligence and human connection, both in our personal lives and in the workplace.

The Way Forward

As we continue to integrate AI and technology into our lives, it is imperative that we do not lose sight of what makes us human. We must prioritize emotional intelligence and genuine connections. This requires a conscious effort to step away from our screens and engage in meaningful interactions. For HR professionals, leaders, and individuals alike, this means fostering environments that value and cultivate emotional intelligence.

While AI and technology offer incredible potential, they should not come at the cost of our humanity. By prioritizing emotional intelligence and true human connection, we can navigate this digital age with empathy and understanding, ensuring that our interactions remain rich and meaningful. My work is dedicated to this cause, and I am deeply committed to helping individuals and teams rediscover the joy and fulfillment that come from genuine human connections. Together, we can create a future where technology enhances, rather than diminishes, our ability to connect, communicate, and collaborate.

CONNECT WITH AMMIE

www.wolfpackhr.com
www.ammiemichaels.com

Resilience Over Adversity

Addressing Domestic Violence and Empowering Survivors

The internet is buzzing with shock and speculation after a video surfaced showing Puffy Daddy allegedly kicking Cassie in the face. This disturbing incident has raised serious concerns about domestic violence.

Every day, countless women around the world experience the harrowing reality of domestic violence. This pervasive issue knows no boundaries, affecting individuals of all backgrounds, ages, and socioeconomic statuses. The staggering statistics reveal a sobering truth about the prevalence of intimate partner violence, underscoring the urgent need for increased awareness, support, and resources to address this widespread and devastating problem.

Triasia Yun-Robinson co- owner/ Director Of Healing & Restoration Consulting LLC , Mamentsl health agency, is a survivor of domestic violence. She states *"as I watched Cassie roll until fall on the floor like a fetus I remember myself in the same position thinking why me.*

Now I stand here and say why not I am not a victim. I am a survivor and because God has granted to see me through I'm able to show other women the resilience we all possess." Triasia Yun- Robinson also owns an organization Lovely Lady Network to help women and young children build their self esteem and self worthiness through education and literacy. *"if I knew my worth, if I loved myself enough,*

I would have been able to not get in a situation that almost killed me." Women need should know that the fit love heals not only themselves but the world ! In the face of the insidious grip of domestic violence, resilience emerges as a powerful force of transformation and healing. As survivors navigate the arduous path to reclaim their lives, their unwavering strength and courage illuminate a path of hope for others. Through community support, awareness, and advocacy, we can collectively work towards a world where resilience triumphs over adversity, and where every individual finds solace, safety, and empowerment.

www.instagram.com/becomingalovelylady

Healingrestorationsconsulting.com

The SHE RISES STUDIOS PODCAST

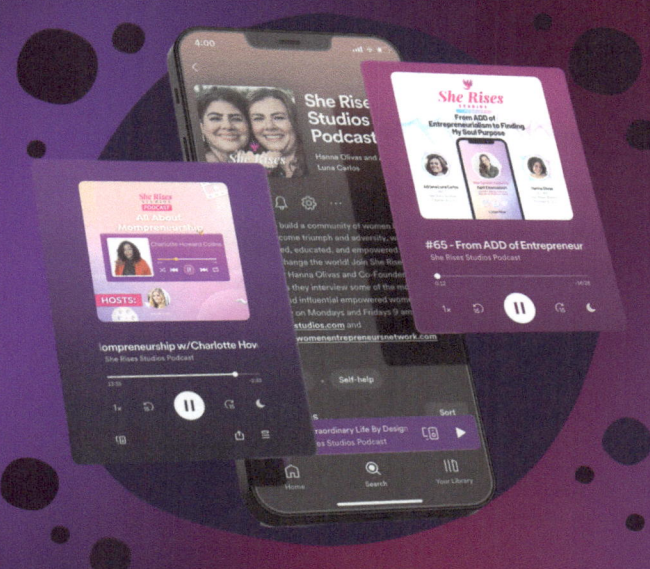

The She Rises Studios podcast is dedicated to empowering women like you to reach their full potential and live their best lives. With inspiring stories, insightful interviews, and practical advice from experts in different industries, our podcast is your go-to source for information, inspiration, and motivation. Join us as we explore topics like:

- Overcoming self-doubt and limiting beliefs
- Building and running a successful business
- Building confidence and Self-esteem
- Navigating career transitions
- Starting and growing a business
- Balancing work and family life
- Improving physical and mental health
- Finding meaning and purpose in life
- So many more

Our guests include successful entrepreneurs, inspiring thought leaders, and everyday women who have overcome challenges and achieved their dreams. Each episode is packed with actionable tips and strategies to help you take your life to the next level.

MELISSA FERRER-BURKE: EMPOWERING WOMEN THROUGH ART AND HEALING AT ELLEVATE HER

by Melissa Ferrer-Burke

In a world where art meets healing, Melissa Ferrer-Burke stands as a visionary leader, passionately dedicated to empowering women through the transformative power of creative expression. As the CEO and *"Visionary-in-Chief"* of **Ellevate Her**, a healing center and foundation launched in 2023, Melissa has cultivated a sanctuary for women to thrive, offering programs that focus on recovery, self-discovery, and personal growth. With a lifetime of personal experience and artistic exploration, Melissa has crafted an environment where art, therapy, and holistic wellness come together to foster healing for single women.

Melissa's journey is one marked by resilience and the determination to turn her personal experiences into something meaningful for others. A trauma survivor herself, she is no stranger to the complexities of healing, and it is this profound understanding that drives her commitment to supporting women on their paths to recovery. *"I passionately believe in the transformative power of the arts to empower women. Throughout my life, I have dedicated myself to supporting women, channeling my own experiences and artistic vision into meaningful action,"* she explains.

The Creation of Ellevate Her: A Lifelong Vision Realized

In the fall of 2023, Melissa launched Ellevate Her, a foundation based in Florida that is more than just a center for healing; it is a sanctuary where women can come together in a nurturing community to learn, grow, and express themselves. For Melissa, the timing of the foundation's launch was deeply personal and symbolic. She attributes much of the center's creation to what she refers to as *"divine timing,"* where all of her life's experiences, education, and global exposure

came together at the right moment to serve others. *"All of my life's experiences and education were able to come together at this time to help others along their healing paths,"* she says, reflecting on the foundation's beginnings.

A Lifetime of Learning and Mentorship

Melissa's journey to becoming a leader in healing and empowerment didn't happen overnight. She acknowledges the importance of mentorship and guidance in her life, having studied healing programs, wellness retreats, and artistic workshops around the world. Each of these experiences was pivotal in shaping the programs offered at Ellevate Her. From art therapy to yoga, breathwork, and even cold plunging, every modality has been personally explored by Melissa on her own path to healing. *"Every program we offer at EH I have personally studied, used, and found helpful along my personal journey,"* she shares. This hands-on approach ensures that the women at Ellevate Her receive authentic, effective support.

Art as a Path to Healing

At the heart of Ellevate Her lies the belief that art can be a powerful tool for healing. The center offers a variety of art therapy sessions designed to provide women with a safe space to express their emotions without the need for words. *"Art therapy can provide a safe environment for authentic expression, an opportunity to 'verbalize' inner emotions without having to talk, can help contain overwhelming emotions, and help reconcile negative feelings,"* Melissa explains. The creative process allows women to connect with their innermost selves, using artistic expression as a means of self-discovery and emotional healing.

The *"Rise, Melissa"* Art Series: A Collaborative Journey of Transformation

Melissa's personal journey of resilience and empowerment is perhaps most vividly captured in her art series, *"Rise, Melissa."* This collection of six artworks is a collaborative effort between Melissa and world-renowned photographer Robert Farber, with whom she has shared both a personal and professional relationship for over 25 years. Their creative partnership, which began in 1999, has produced a body of work that seamlessly blends photography and painting to tell a compelling narrative of transformation.

"Combining my true emotion and his elegant lens, we were able to connect sight and feeling as subject and photographer," Melissa reflects on the collaboration. The *"Rise, Melissa"* series takes viewers on a powerful journey of growth, resilience, and self-discovery, using vivid colors and evocative imagery to convey the emotional experiences Melissa has encountered throughout her life.

Building a Community of Empowerment

While art is central to the work at Ellevate Her, Melissa believes that the true strength of the foundation lies in its community. *"You're only as strong as your team. In one word, community,"* she emphasizes. The center is designed to be a supportive environment where women can heal and grow together. The women at Ellevate Her come from diverse backgrounds, but they are united by a shared mission of healing and empowerment.

The success of the foundation's programs is a testament to Melissa's holistic approach. Whether it's through art therapy, life coaching, or physical practices like yoga and breathwork, the programs at Ellevate Her are tailored to each individual. *"Each individual is unique. We at EH are proud to say that we cater programs to each specific case,"* Melissa explains. This personalized approach has led to life-changing transformations for many of the women who have participated.

The Power of Collaboration and Knowledge Sharing

For Melissa, collaboration is key to creating a thriving community. She believes that every woman has unique skills and experiences to offer, and that by learning from one another, they can become stronger. *"Knowledge is power. We all have such a unique set of skills. We learn from each other and are always stronger together and united,"* she says.

Melissa's dedication to this philosophy extends beyond the walls of Ellevate Her. She envisions the foundation as a global movement, connecting women from around the world who share a common goal of healing and personal expansion. Already, she is working to bridge her home base in South Florida with Florence, Italy, providing opportunities for international education and collaboration.

Looking to the Future

As Ellevate Her continues to grow, Melissa's vision for the future is expansive. *"I see EH building centers globally,"* she says, envisioning a network of healing centers that empower women worldwide. Her goal is to create spaces where women can connect, heal, and learn from one another, transcending geographical boundaries to build a global sisterhood of support and empowerment.

Through her unwavering dedication, Melissa Ferrer-Burke is not only transforming the lives of the women she serves, but also demonstrating the profound impact that art and community can have on the healing process. Ellevate Her is a reflection of her life's work—an ongoing journey of resilience, empowerment, and creativity that continues to inspire women to rise to their fullest potential.

CONNECT WITH MELISSA
www.instagram.com/ellevate_her
www.linkedin.com/company/ellevate-her/about
www.ellevateher.org

Photo Credits: Rosina Di Bello
@rosinadibellophoto

PRIORITIZE SELF-CARE TO THRIVE: INSIGHTS FROM JENNIFER & NATASHA

by Jennifer Griffith and Natasha Ganes

In today's fast-paced world, stress has become an unavoidable part of life. However, prolonged stress can lead to burnout, affecting our mental, physical, and emotional well-being. Jennifer Griffith and Natasha Ganes, co-creators of *"In the Life of Zen"* and hosts of the "Where Money Meets Soul" podcast, understand the importance of prioritizing self-care to avoid burnout and thrive in every aspect of life.

Drawing from their combined expertise in health, wellness, and professional development, Jennifer and Natasha offer valuable insights into the transformative power of self-care. Through their own personal journeys, they have discovered the profound impact that prioritizing self-care can have on overall well-being.

Natasha's Story resonates with many individuals who find themselves juggling multiple responsibilities and struggling to manage stress effectively. As a busy woman with numerous commitments, Natasha understands the challenges of balancing career, family, and personal goals. At one point, stress consumed her life, leaving her overwhelmed and exhausted. However, through prioritizing self-care, Natasha was able to regain control of her life and find fulfillment.

Similarly, Jennifer's Story highlights the dangers of neglecting self-care in pursuit of productivity. As someone who thrives on constant activity and achievement, Jennifer found herself on the brink of burnout after years of relentless work. Recognizing the importance of self-care, Jennifer embarked on a journey of self-discovery and transformation, reclaiming her health and happiness in the process.

Stress, overwhelm, and burnout are common experiences in today's society, but Jennifer and Natasha emphasize the importance of recognizing the signs and taking proactive steps to prioritize self-care. By incorporating self-care practices into daily routines, individuals can protect their mental and physical health, enhance productivity, and cultivate a greater sense of well-being.

To avoid burnout and thrive in life, Jennifer and Natasha offer practical tips for prioritizing self-care:

1. **Write Down Everything You Need to Do and Learn to Delegate:** By creating a list of tasks and prioritizing them, individuals can identify areas where they can delegate or eliminate tasks that are not essential.

2. **Accept Your Emotions and Change Your Perspective:** Instead of dwelling on negative thoughts and emotions, practice gratitude and focus on positive aspects of life.

3. **Create Boundaries and Stick with Them:** Learn to say no to commitments that are not aligned with your priorities, and establish healthy boundaries to protect your time and energy.

4. **Exercise:** Incorporate regular physical activity into your routine to reduce stress, boost mood, and improve overall health.

5. **Practice Mindfulness:** Take time to quiet the mind and focus on the present moment through meditation, deep breathing, or other mindfulness practices.

6. **Try Something New:** Step out of your comfort zone and engage in activities that bring joy and fulfillment, whether it's learning a new hobby or exploring new experiences.

7. **Take a Digital Detox:** Disconnect from electronic devices periodically to reduce screen time and promote relaxation.

8. **Meditate:** Set aside time for meditation or guided relaxation to calm the mind and reduce stress.

9. **Prioritize Sleep:** Ensure adequate rest by establishing a bedtime routine and creating a conducive sleep environment.

By incorporating these self-care practices into daily life, individuals can protect their well-being, enhance resilience, and unlock their full potential. Jennifer and Natasha's message is clear: prioritizing self-care is not selfish; it's essential for living a balanced, fulfilling life.

Through their platform, *"In the Life of Zen,"* Jennifer and Natasha share their experiences and insights to empower others to prioritize self-care and create the life of their dreams. By embracing self-care as a non-negotiable aspect of life, individuals can cultivate greater happiness, resilience, and overall well-being.

In the journey of life, self-care is the key to unlocking our full potential and living with purpose and passion. With Jennifer and Natasha's guidance, individuals can embark on a transformative journey of self-discovery, empowerment, and holistic well-being.

BLESSED BEYOND STRESS: ANNA LUGO'S PATH TO BUILDING PURE TEA LOVE AND PURE CBD LUV

Anna Lugo is the visionary behind Pure Tea Love and Pure CBD Luv, two brands that blend wellness with faith, offering natural solutions to common ailments like anxiety, chronic pain, and sleeplessness. Her entrepreneurial journey is deeply rooted in personal experiences and a strong sense of purpose, driven by love for her family and a passion for helping others.

The inspiration for Pure CBD Luv came on a deeply emotional and significant day—November 11, 2020, the birthday of her father, a proud veteran who served in the Army. During the uncertainties of the COVID-19 pandemic, Anna was grappling with anxiety, inflammation, and insomnia, particularly following the traumatic event of her daughter being struck by a drunk driver and sustaining a brain bleed. It was in this challenging period that Anna discovered CBD as a natural remedy, and it quickly became an essential part of her daily routine. Realizing that she needed a consistent way to take her doses, she decided to launch Pure CBD Luv as a tribute to her father's legacy.

Two years later, Anna expanded her vision by creating Pure Tea Love, launched on February 22, 2022, which also holds a personal connection. This time, the brand honored her late grandfather, affectionately known as Poppa Georgie, who was born on George Washington's birthday.

Both brands reflect Anna's values of faith, positivity, and healing, with the slogan *"We have a tea for that... Positivity!"* emphasizing the focus on wellness and natural solutions. *"We are more than a wellness company,"* Anna says, *"We are Healers, not Dealers,"* and she firmly believes that CBD is *"Hope, not Dope."*

Anna's extensive career in IT and her role as a Tea'V Host have greatly influenced the development of her business ventures. With over 40 years of experience in the corporate world, Anna has honed her leadership skills and gained valuable insights into navigating successes and failures. Participating in mentorship programs since the 1980s has been integral to her personal growth and business acumen. She credits her ability to present confidently to top executives and her constant drive for learning as key factors in her entrepreneurial success. Her background in IT also helped her build a strong social media presence, where she can inspire others. *"Inspiring others to be their best self is way better than building complex data networks,"* Anna reflects.

Her motto, *"I'm Too Blessed to Be Stressed,"* reflects her deep faith and personal approach to life's challenges. In her first book, Anna writes about her philosophy in the chapter titled *"Spirituali-Tea' is my Priori-Tea', for Eterni-Tea."* For Anna, worrying is a form of spiritual dissonance, as it offends her faith in God's plan. By choosing positivity, she aligns herself with divine trust, believing that every trial is an opportunity for growth. Her motto is a reminder to keep faith strong, no matter the obstacles.

One of the most impactful moments in Anna's journey occurred in 2023, when her *"Up2UGod"* TikTok page reached 2.7 million people on Facebook, followed by the sudden loss of access to her page. Undeterred, she pivoted to TikTok, where she began posting *"license plates with a worship song attached."* As a *"License Plate Whisper,"* Anna interprets the spiritual messages behind the license plates she encounters, often feeling called to pray for others or share messages of hope. This unique interest has led to many profound connections, and Anna is working on a book that will tell the stories behind these signs.

Through her businesses, social media presence, and unwavering faith, Anna Lugo continues to inspire, uplift, and connect with people worldwide. Her journey is a testament to the power of resilience, faith, and the healing potential of natural wellness solutions.

CONNECT WITH ANNA

www.women-inspiring-women-and-men-too.ueniweb.com
www.puretealove.com
www.instagram.com/purecbdluv
1-725-221-1511
puretealove@yahoo.com

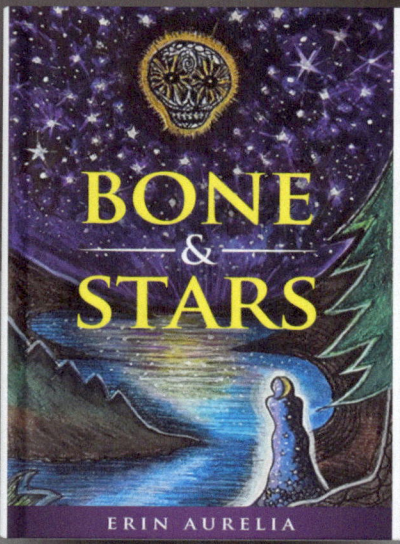

BONE & STARS
by Erin Aurelia

Bone & Stars is a powerful poetry collection that traces one woman's journey from silence and emotional abuse to liberation and self-reclamation. These poems delve into the raw determination to truly live—not as someone numbed by denial, but as a whole, defiant, and shining self. Through vivid, unflinching verses, the author explores escaping an abusive marriage, healing unseen wounds, and finding her voice to rise like a phoenix, unapologetic and fierce.

This collection offers solace and recognition to those who have endured emotional abuse, providing a mirror for experiences often dismissed because they leave no visible scars. It is a testament to the resilience of the spirit and a reminder that recovery and self-empowerment are possible. Bone & Stars is an anthem for anyone seeking to break free, heal, and shine as the center of their own universe.

HEALING JOURNAL FOR WARRIOR WOMEN
by Marika Wessels

Healing Journal for Warrior Women is your companion for growth, resilience, and self-discovery. Designed to empower your journey, this guided journal combines mindfulness exercises, reflective prompts, and uplifting affirmations to help you navigate challenges, embrace your inner strength, and cultivate self-love. Whether you're healing from past wounds, reclaiming your voice, or seeking balance, this journal provides the tools and inspiration to transform pain into power. Let this be your safe space to reflect, recharge, and rise as the warrior woman you are.

AVAILABLE ON AMAZON

PUBLISHED BY SHE RISES STUDIOS
www.SheRisesStudios.com

THE POWER OF PUBLISHING
WHY PUBLISH A BOOK, YOU ASK?

Publishing a book is one of the most fulfilling ways to share your story with the world and leave a lasting legacy. It boosts your credibility and highlights your expertise in your industry. Plus, you'll be stepping into the massive $138.5 billion book market industry —and it's still growing!

Best of all, it's easier now than ever before to get your book out there. How exciting is that?

At She Rises Studios, we are on a mission to become the top publishing house for women in the USA. We believe in the power of storytelling to create influencers and stronger communities. We're here to help you break barriers, grow, and make waves in the publishing world.

Get published with us TODAY!
Visit www.SheRisesStudios.com or email us at
contact@sherisesstudios.com